CASTLES OF CALIFORNIA

Publications of the North American Jules Verne Society

The Palik Series (edited by Brian Taves)

The Marriage of a Marquis
Contributors: Edward Baxter, Jean-Michel Margot, Walter James Miller, Kieran M. O'Driscoll, Brian Taves

Shipwrecked Family: Marooned with Uncle Robinson
Translated by Sidney Kravitz; Introduction by Brian Taves

Mr. Chimp & Other Plays
Translated by Frank Morlock; Introduction by Jean-Michel Margot

The Count of Chanteleine: A Tale of the French Revolution
Translated by Edward Baxter; Introduction by Brian Taves; Notes by Garmt de Vries-Uiterweerd, Volker Dehs

Vice, Redemption, and the Distant Colony
Translated, with notes, by Kieran M. O'Driscoll

Around the World in 80 Days: The 1874 Play
Contributors: Philippe Burgaud, Jean-Louis Trudel, Jean-Michel Margot, Brian Taves

Bandits & Rebels
Translated by Edward Baxter; Introduction by Daniel Compère

Golden Danube
Translated, with notes, by Kieran M. O'Driscoll

A Priest in 1835
Translated, with and introductory essay and notes, by Daniéle Chatelain and George Slusser

(Other volumes in preparation)

Editorial Committee of the North American Jules Verne Society:
Brian Taves, Jean-Michel Margot, Terry Harpold

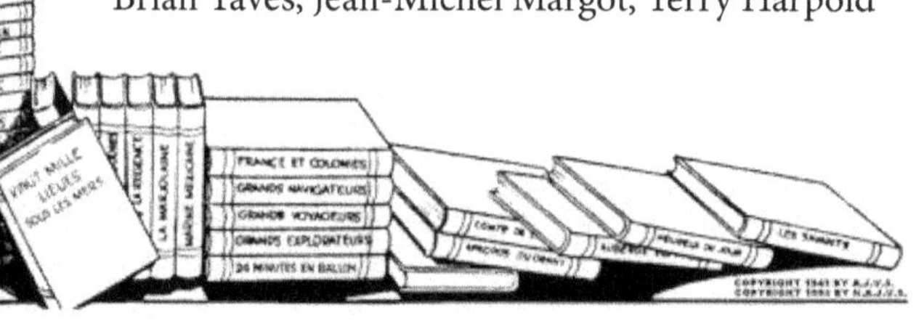

CASTLES OF CALIFORNIA

Two Plays by Jules Verne

Translated, with an introduction
and notes, by

Kieran M. O'Driscoll

Edited and with an afterword by Brian Taves

for the North American Jules Verne Society

The Palik Series

BearManor Fiction

2017

Castles of California
by Jules Verne

For information, address:

BearManor Fiction
P. O. Box 71426
Albany, GA 31708

bearmanormedia.com

North American Jules Verne Society: najvs.org

Typesetting and layout by John Teehan

Published in the USA by BearManor Media

ISBN — 978-1-62933-126-3

Table of Contents

For John, Neil, Alice and Aiden, with much love.
And for Allan Carlos Trindade da Silva,
student and friend.

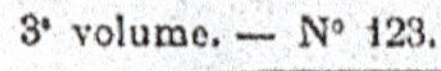

3e volume. — No 123. 10 c. Un an : 6 fr.

LES HOMMES D'AUJOURD'HUI

DESSINS DE GILL

BUREAUX : 48, RUE MONSIEUR LE PRINCE, PARIS

JULES VERNE

Jules Verne would ultimately be acclaimed as much for conquering the stage as a writer of novels.

Introduction

by Kieran O'Driscoll

Jules Verne's writings for the theater were his first series of major fictional creations prior to his embarking on the prodigious series of novels in his "Extraordinary Journeys into the Known and Unknown Worlds" for which he is most remembered today.[1] Through the study of Verne's theatrical works, a more balanced critical judgement can be reached regarding an author who has been so often fundamentally misunderstood. The plays prove, for instance, that Verne was hardly a children's writer, nor simply an anticipator of future technological and scientific developments. Nor was he a conformist middle-class gentleman offering few surprises in his writings, a writer far removed from any hint of sexual themes or sauciness in his works. The only remaining truism from amongst this list of Vernian stereotypes which has not been demolished, and which remains standing and intact, is that of a novelist who specialized in themes of adventure, science and travel, journeys into the far-flung corners of the globe (and its interior!) and into outer space. An article by Verne scholar Robert Pourvoyeur argues, however, that even this reasonably accurate image of Jules Verne's identity as a writer can be challenged if we delve more deeply into the perseverance of his love for the theater; a love which

1. The North American Jules Verne Society has devoted much of its publication efforts to revealing this fact, first with *Journey Through the Impossible* (Amherst, NY: Prometheus, 2003), and in the Palik Series, *Mr. Chimp & Other Plays* (Albany: GA: BearManor Fiction, 2011), *Around the World in 80 Days—The 1874 Play* (Albany, GA: BearManor Fiction, 2013), and the present volume.

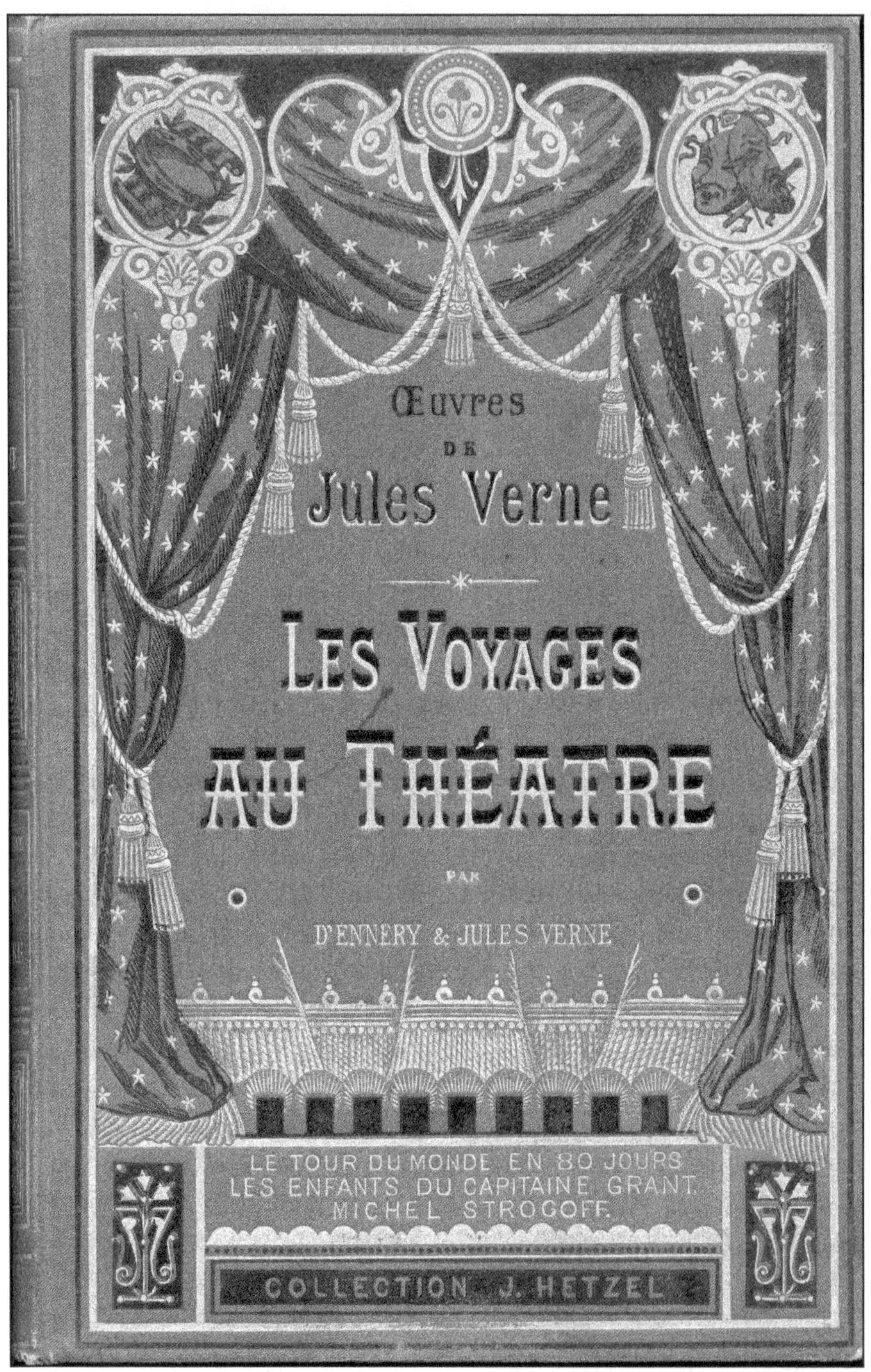

The cover of the 1881 Hetzel publication of Verne's stage versions of his three most famous novels, *Around the World in Eighty Days*, *Michael Strogoff*, and *The Children of Captain Grant.*

is indeed so persistent that it begs the question as to whether or not theatrical writing might not have been Verne's true passion, indeed his true vocation.

Of course, as Pourvoyeur goes on to immediately acknowledge, a theme such as "Jules Verne and the theater" is not instantly obvious as a central Vernian preoccupation, given that his novels, which he began writing in earnest and most successfully in his thirties, have significantly overshadowed the plays written by him, alone or in collaboration with others, not only in his twenties but indeed, even as far back as his childhood. Jules Verne contributed so prolifically to the theater that when we examine his theatrical output, in Pourvoyeur's words, "there is so much to say about this issue."

Pourvoyeur, in his preface to a 1979 volume which contained the Verne novel *Clovis Dardentor* as well as the play *Un neveu d'Amérique ou Les Deux Frontignac* (*A Nephew from America, or, the Two Frontignacs*), divides Verne's plays into four broad categories: the "spoken theatrical works of his youth" (of which the two United States-themed plays in the present volume are representative); his operatic works in which he wrote librettos to accompany the music of various composers; his plays based on novels from his series of "Extraordinary Journeys;" and, finally, theatrical-style writing within his novels themselves.[2] Since that time, one additional play was discovered that defies any of these categories, an original pastiche written directly for the theater but involving characters from his novels: *Voyage à travers l'impossible* (*Journey Through the Impossible*, 1882).

The two plays—*The Castles of California* and *A Nephew from America*—which have been translated for the first time in this volume of the Palik Series, belong to the first category identified by Pourvoyeur. Thus, I will speak generally about the early spoken plays written by Jules Verne as a young man in his twenties, living in Paris and working in the theater, and I will then speak specifically about the two particular plays here. Both have been selected because of their intrinsic interest to a readership based in the United States, given that they both deal with sojourns in the United States as a significant part of their story.

Verne's first foray into "spoken theater," as Pourvoyeur calls it, was a play written during his childhood, at the time of his unrequited

2. Jules Verne, *Clovis Dardentor*, collection "10/18" (Paris: UGE, 1979).

Journey Through the Impossible (1882).

love for his cousin Caroline, when he wrote a tragedy in verse which was refused by the Riquiqui puppet theater in his native Nantes. Not discouraged, Verne continued to fill his school copybooks with further plays throughout the remainder of his childhood and teenage years and on into his twenties. These plays were generally either tragedies or "vaudeville"-type offerings (comedies or farces). We know little of the exact dates of these early attempts at writing for the theater, apart from what Jules Verne's grandson, Jean-Jules Verne, has later written on this subject, in his biography of the author. Pourvoyeur acknowledges that these plays are of little intrinsic value, but reading them is enlightening in the interpretation of the later novels.

Indeed, as shall be shown later in this Introduction, the themes of greed, vanity, pride and materialism, which are satirized in the two plays of this volume, were taken up again by Verne later in his writing career, in such novels as *La Chasse au Météore* (*The Hunt for the Meteor*, 1908).

Verne arrived in Paris to study law in 1848, at the age of twenty, but his heart lay in becoming involved, as quickly as possible, in the world of Parisian theater. Having secured an introduction to Alexandre Dumas *père,* his meeting with this illustrious French writer marked the beginning of a lifetime friendship. Dumas was to have a lasting influence on Verne, and the bond was such that, forty years after this first meeting, Dumas *fils* would inform Verne in a letter that it was Jules Verne, rather than Dumas *fils,* who was the true son of Dumas. The influence of Dumas *père* on a young Jules Verne began when the latter, working as a voluntary secretary at the Théâtre Historique in Paris, watched with wondrous admiration, in the box reserved for Dumas himself, a performance of the Dumas play *La Jeunesse des Mousquetaires* (*The Musketeers' Youth*, 1849).

Though Verne had by now graduated in law, and was originally destined to follow in his father's footsteps by taking over the family legal practice in Nantes, his burning ambition was to work in and write for the theater, and it was in 1850 that his light comedy play *Les Pailles Rompues* (*Broken Straws*) was performed for the first time on the Parisian stage. This was the story of a flirtatious woman and her jealous husband; similarly, the two plays appearing in this volume are also romantic comedies, one of which (*A Nephew from America*) features just such a jealous, suspicious husband in the person of the hapless Roquamor, and a flirtatious wife in the person of his coquettish spouse Antonia. Verne dedicated *Broken Straws* to Dumas *père*, whose experience and advice, he acknowledged, had been of undoubted assistance. *Broken Straws* was a successful example of the genre known as "marivaudage": a work espousing themes of light-hearted gallantry, the term being derived from the eponymous French dramatist Marivaud, who was, therefore, along with Dumas, another influence on Verne, as was Musset, whose impact on Verne can be discerned in the play *Monna Lisa* (1851), originally entitled *Léonard de Vinci.* In this comic play, written in verse in collaboration with the librettist Michel Carré, da Vinci loves but loses the beautiful Mona Lisa, whose portrait he is painting, because, ironically, he becomes so absorbed by his art as to pay no romantic attention to the lovely subject of his masterpiece.[3] Pourvoyeur claims that da Vinci's terrible awkwardness in love "illuminates the psychology of the shy introvert which Verne was."[4]

Les Châteaux en Californie ou Pierre qui roule n'amasse pas mousse (*The Castles of California, or, A Rolling Stone Gathers No Moss*), although never staged, became Verne's first published play. Beginning in 1851, two novellas and one short story by Verne appeared in the journal *Musée des Familles* (*Family Museum*). These were *Les premiers navires de la marine mexicaine* (*The First Ships of the Mexican Navy*, July 1851), "Un voyage en ballon" (August 1851, and translated as "A Voyage in a Balloon" in *Sartain's Union Magazine of Literature and Art* in Philadelphia, May 1852), and *Martin Paz* (serialized in *Family Museum* from July through August 1852, and translated as *The Pearl of Lima--A Story of True Love* in *Graham's Magazine* in Philadelphia, April 1853[5]). *The Castles of California*, also written at this time, became Verne's fourth appearance in *Family Museum*, published over fifteen pages in the September 1852 issue. Editor of *Family Museum*, and providing encouragement to the novice Verne, was Pierre-Michel-François Chevalier (1812-1860), a fellow native of Nantes. Pitre-Chevalier would accept two more novellas by Verne while at *Family Museum*, a magazine with a monthly circulation of 30,000 around this time. Pitre-Chevalier partly collaborated on *The Castles of California*, and it was highly topical; in 1846, settlers had rebelled against control by Mexico to create an independent republic, and two years later California had become part of the United States, even as gold was discovered and the rush of "forty-niners" from around the globe began. When gold was again discovered in North America, in the Klondike in 1896, Verne wrote a novel of the struggle for riches and

3. *Monna Lisa*, translated into English for the first time, will be included in the upcoming Palik series volume, *Worlds Known and Unknown*.

4. For more on Verne's sexuality and undertones in some of his writing, see my Introduction to another Verne novel in the Palik series, *Golden Danube* (Albany, GA: BearManor Fiction, 2014).

5. This translation of the original magazine text of *Martin Paz* was included as an appendix in the Palik series volume, *Bandits & Rebels* (Albany, GA: BearManor Fiction, 2014). Other translations and appearances in English of *Martin Paz* were from the revised text later published by Hetzel in 1875.

Pitre-Chevalier, editor of the magazine *Family Museum*, who published Verne's earliest stories and *The Castles of California*.

survival in the region, *The Golden Volcano*, eventually published in 1906.[6]

Verne went on to write other plays, mostly in the comic "vaudeville" style, but these were largely consigned to oblivion from the time of their creation right up to the present day, an oversight the Palik Series assists in rectifying. Verne spent a long time developing his writing style, a style which came to fruition when he found his niche in the novels of exploration and scientific anticipation for which he is best known. While seeking to find that thematic specialization, he had initially hesitated between different literary genres, from spoken plays to librettos to short stories and, ultimately, novels. The quality of such plays as *A Nephew from America* testifies to the calibre of playwright which Jules Verne might have become with a little more experience and had he not definitively opted to devote the rest of his life and writing career to his "long travels throughout the known and unknown worlds," per Pourvoyeur.

Before examining the themes of the two plays presented in first-time English translation in this volume, it is worth noting that one, *A Nephew from America,* was not written by Jules Verne alone, but rather in collaboration with his fellow French playwright Edouard Cadol (despite the fact that, in the French original version of this play, only Verne is credited). Cadol (1831-1898) was not alone in collaborating on the creation of this play in its published forms, but its original draft version was partly the work of yet another playwright, Charles Wallut. How, then, did this collaboration between Verne and the ultimately uncredited Cadol—and the prior, equally uncredited involvement of Wallut—come about?

In about 1871 or 1872, Jules Verne was introduced to another French dramatist, Edouard Cadol, by Madame Larochelle, the wife of Paul Larochelle, who was, at that time, the director of the Théâtre Cluny in Paris, and who had been responsible for "discovering" this new playwright, Cadol, in around 1867 or 1868. An initial collaborative project between Verne and Cadol, their theatrical adaptation of

---

6. "Anon., "Jules Verne's Hundredth Book." *The Commercial Appeal* (Memphis, Tennessee), November 30, 1902. *The Golden Volcano* was first translated by I.O. Evans in two volumes, *The Claim on Forty Mile Creek* and *Flood and Flame*, published in 1962, from the 1906 revision by Michel Verne; Jules's original text, only discovered in the 1980s, was translated by Edward Baxter in 2008 as *The Golden Volcano*.

Edouard Cadol

Verne's story *Voyages et Aventures du Capitaine Hatteras* (*Journeys and Adventures of Captain Hatteras,* 1866), ultimately foundered because of the resistance to the project by the various Parisian theater managers to whom it was proposed. Verne therefore suggested to Cadol that they work together on Verne's planned play *Le Tour du monde en quatre-vingts jours* (*Around the World in Eighty Days*), simultaneously announcing his (Verne's) intention to also publish this story as a novel. Having discussed the general plan for a stage adaptation of *Around the World in Eighty Days* with Cadol, Verne then sent Cadol a "developed script" which was subsequently fine-tuned and written in a finalized version for stage performance by Cadol himself, and lastly, corrected

Théâtre Cluny, where *A Nephew from America* was performed.

by Verne. The collaboration between both dramatists proved difficult, and in March, 1872, Verne began to write the novelized version of *Around the World in Eighty Days*, which was ultimately published—to resounding and lasting success—at the end of that same year.

The French press then announced that the play, under its original French title *Le Tour du monde en quatre-vingts jours,* was about to be performed publicly at the Théâtre Cluny, but it was subsequently rejected by that theater's manager, Paul Larochelle, who then, it seems, asked Verne to have some other previously unpublished and unperformed

The final and very successful 1874 stage creation of *Around the World in 80 Days* involved a collaboration between Verne and d'Ennery, not Cadol.

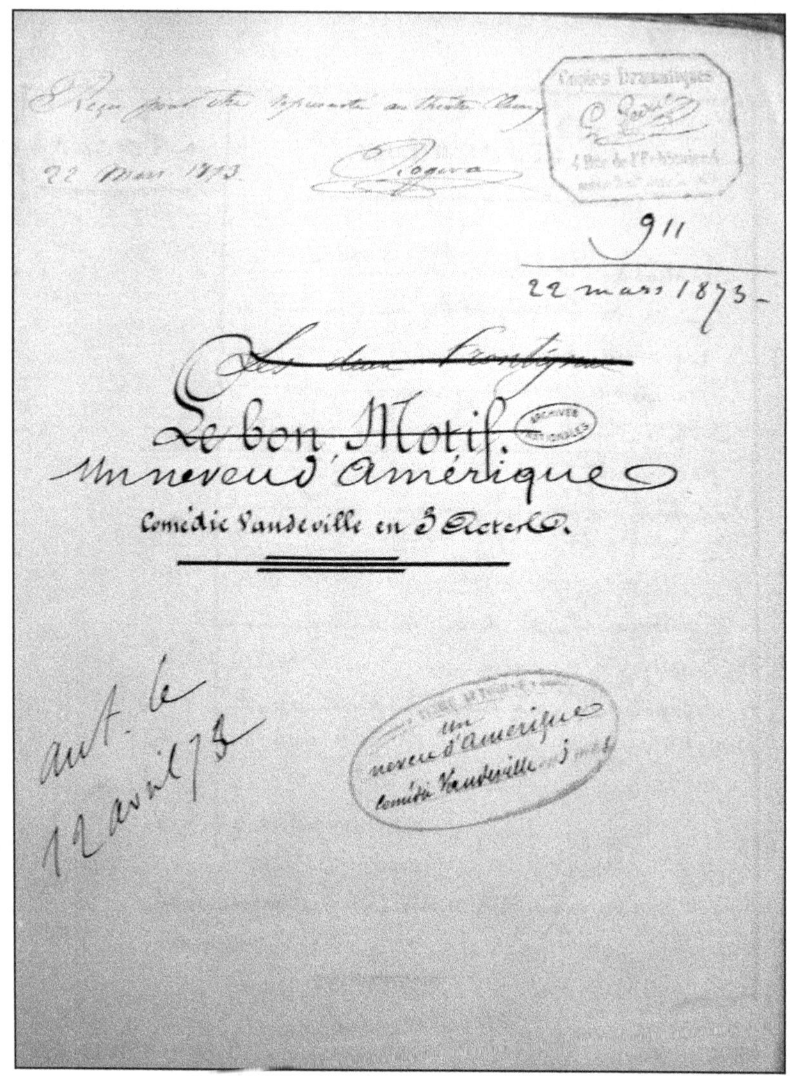

Cover of the original manuscript of *A Nephew from America*, with the title change.

play of his staged instead of *Around the World in Eighty Days*. The purpose of this proposition may have been to compensate Cadol for the failure to stage the latter play on which he had completed so much work, or to capitalize on the significant interest of the Parisian theater-going public in a play written by Jules Verne—or, indeed, perhaps for both reasons. (In turn, Verne would shortly join with a new collaborator, Adolphe d'Ennery, instead of Cadol, to turn the novel *Around the*

World in Eighty Days into an extraordinarily successful play.)[7]

Verne thus chose a play entitled *Le Bon Motif* (*The Right Motive*), which he had co-written with Charles Wallut (1829-1899) around 1861, but which had never seen the light of day up to that point. Cadol was thus commissioned to rework that play. Though the extent of Cadol's reworking of the play is unknown, it seems unlikely that it involved any major rewriting, given that he had only a few short weeks to complete his task.

This play was accepted, but its original working title *The Right Motive* was rejected by the censors and, in its place, two alternative titles were suggested: *The Two Frontignacs* or *A Nephew from America.* The latter title is visible on the original manuscript of the play which has been deposited in the archives of the Censor's office.

In order to help finance the launch of this play, Cadol tried to interest an insurance company in providing funds for the programme of the play. However, Verne's publisher, Hetzel, did not agree to this proposed arrangement, as he insisted that he was the sole publisher of any book authored by Jules Verne. Verne suggested removing his name from the work, in order to allow Cadol's initial project to come to fruition, but this proposal was rejected this time by Larochelle, who insisted that the play must appear under the authorship of Jules Verne. Even though the newspapers of the time were aware of Cadol's participation in the writing of *A Nephew from America,* Cadol seems to have voluntarily withdrawn his name from the authorship credits, and so it was that the play was performed, and the script published, under Verne's name only.

The play did not prove very successful. It closed after only fifty-eight performances, and the authors' royalties were divided equally between Verne, Wallut and Cadol, each of whom received the sum of 423.97 francs for their respective contributions. It was, however, the only Verne play issued by Hetzel other than those from the "Extraordinary Journeys."

Having discussed the turbulent genesis of *A Nephew from America,* let us now examine, more specifically, the themes of the two plays presented in this edition. In discussing their themes and language, I

7. For the Verne-d'Ennery version, and a full analysis of the background of both plays and the novel, see the Palik series volume, *Around the World in 80 Days—The 1874 Play.*

shall also take account of Pourvoyeur's (very positive) evaluations of these two pieces. Readers who do not wish to learn details of the plots of the two pieces presented in this volume may prefer to read the rest of this Introduction after having first read the plays themselves.

A Nephew from America belongs to the genre of light romantic comedy, and is a satire of materialism and social climbing, which links it thematically with the other play translated in these pages, *The Castles of California*. *A Nephew from America* begins with a magnificent high-society ball given by Roquamor (apparently on the urging of his wife Antonia) at his home in Paris, marking his return to Parisian society after three years spent in Marseille, where he has been concluding various property transactions; we thus learn that he is an investor. Much to his chagrin and frustration, Roquamor is a perfect stranger to all of his guests and is jostled roughly and spoken to rudely, being eventually assumed by some of the guests to be a "casual domestic" hired for the occasion. He is portrayed as a figure of comic ineptitude; he is also described as a "madly jealous" husband who is furious at the compliments he overhears being paid to his wife Antonia, whom he (rightly, as it turns out) suspects of being unfaithful to him. She has, we learn, been exchanging declarations of love with one of the main characters, Stanislas de Frontignac, present at this ball, a forty-something social butterfly and "Don Juan" of note, whose selfish, bachelor lifestyle is suddenly and radically overturned when he discovers that he has a nephew, of whose existence he had, up to now, been blissfully unaware. Frontignac is an inveterate womanizer and is full of false flattery in his hyperbolic compliments to the various beautiful women present at this ball.

Marcandier, another guest at this ball, is, like Roquamor, suffering from frustration, but for a different reason—ten years prior to the events of this story, he had contracted a life annuity investment policy with Frontignac, under the terms of which the latter paid a lump sum to the insurance company run by Marcandier, in exchange for a yearly annuity thereafter from the company until his death. Marcandier, when signing the policy, had not expected Frontignac to live very long, as he had been in quite poor health at the time. Ten years later, however, Frontignac enjoys rude good health and Marcandier, another figure of comic haplessness, is seen to seek, unsuccessfully, to cause Frontignac to develop a fatal case of tuberculosis or pneumonia, so as to avoid having to continue to pay him.

At the ball, Stanislas de Frontignac encounters the nephew of whose existence he had known nothing. Stanislas and Savinien de Frontignac, when they bump into each other, trade insults and end up challenging each other to a duel. Upon their exchange of cards, they discover, to the astonishment of both, that they are uncle and nephew. Frontignac Senior had known that his brother had died twenty years previously in the United States, but had not been aware that he had been married, nor that he had left an infant son. Savinien, the eponymous nephew who has travelled from the United States to France, is in love with Madeleine, niece of Carbonnel, and requests the assistance of his uncle in persuading Madeleine's uncle to consent to their marriage, despite the distinct lack of financial security of the young couple. Frontignac Senior, who is forced to reappraise his formerly selfish and hedonistic values upon the discovery of this nephew for whom he feels, despite himself, a certain degree of affection, resolves to do as much as he possibly can to provide for his nephew's future and to help secure his marriage to Madeleine. Carbonnel—similarly to Marcandier—refuses at first to agree to the proposed marriage because of Savinien's having no savings, so that Verne satirises, throughout this play, the "money-grabbing," materialistic, self-interested attitudes of several characters who move in professional, bourgeois Parisian circles, much as he also did in the unfinished 1847 novel, *Jédédias Jamet ou L'Histoire d'une succession* (*Jédédias Jamet or the Tale of an Inheritance*).[8] As well as providing much enjoyment to his readers and viewers of his plays, through his lampooning of these materialistic and self-obsessed fictional characters, Verne is also drawing from his real-life knowledge of the world of the law and stock market, in which he worked while trying to establish himself within the theater.

Another (minor) character who is seen to be quite greedy, mercenary and self-seeking is that of Dominique, the valet of Frontignac Senior. Dominique resents the sudden intrusion of Savinien into the life of his master, as he perceives this long-lost nephew as a potential threat to his prospects of inheriting some of his employer's fortune.

We first become aware of the character of Dominique when Frontignac (the uncle) informs him that he has invited his newfound nephew to lunch and asks his valet to make the necessary preparations;

8. Translated into English for the first time in the first volume of the Palik Series, *The Marriage of a Marquis* (Albany, GA: BearManor Fiction, 2011).

the manservant is clearly discomfited and unhappy at this unexpected piece of news of the arrival of a family member in the life of a man who had hitherto appeared to have no living relations. Frontignac himself, at this point, has not yet come round to feeling any real affection for his nephew, instead saying to his valet, "One has obligations towards members of one's family, I accept that! Let us do things properly, but without any enthusiasm." Dominique, in one of several sarcastic asides, reflects: "As if he couldn't have just stayed where he was in America, that fellow." During their lunch together, uncle and nephew begin to appreciate each other; the uncle reflects that "since I've had to inherit a long-lost nephew, it might as well be this fellow as any other." The nephew simultaneously says to himself that his uncle is "quite an eccentric fellow … but a good man at the back of it all." Savinien does not want to be the cause of any disruption to his uncle's existence: "I don't wish to disturb your routine in any way." He seeks nothing but his uncle's companionship and, indeed, appears thoroughly genuine, and seeking to marry for real love.

The uncle appears to thaw further towards his nephew once it becomes evident that the latter is sincerely seeking his companionship and not any personal financial gain. Indeed, Savinien is adamant that he will not accept money from his uncle, but when the latter declares "I'd like to be able to do something for you," Savinien realizes that "there is still one big favor you *can* do for me": there is "a certain young lady" whom he ardently wishes to marry. The uncle is initially taken aback at his nephew's declaration of unselfish romantic love and the idea of winning a woman's heart through noble, virtuous means ("Enroll in my school and I'll help you cultivate other types [of intentions]," Frontignac Senior roguishly declares.) He agrees to intercede with Monsieur Carbonnel, Madeleine's uncle, on Savinien's behalf, to try to secure his agreement to the marriage of the young lovers. Because of the uncle's long years of selfish manipulation of women (which we infer from his declarations and the poor opinion of him held by other male characters in the play), he sees this attempt to secure the marriage of his nephew as a type of business transaction. He tries to railroad Carbonnel into giving his consent, but when the latter realizes that neither of the two Frontignac gentlemen have much in the way of a dowry to offer his niece, he withdraws his consent, leaving the young couple bereft.

Faced with Savinien's incomprehension of the reasons for Carbonnel's refusal, the uncle admits that he has invested his entire fortune in a life annuity policy, never suspecting that he might one day have to consider the well-being and future of anybody but himself as a single man and a self-professed "selfish cad." The uncle now feels genuine remorse at the thought that he can do nothing in the way of some small financial sacrifice which might have ensured the happiness and security of his nephew. Yet even at this news, Savinien, with his characteristic lack of self-interest or materialism, assures his uncle that "All I ask of you is your affection, and nothing more." The idea then occurs to the uncle to consult with his solicitor in order to see about changing his life annuity policy so that he may be able, after all, to provide for his nephew's security. By now, the uncle realizes that he truly loves his nephew and will do whatever is necessary to ensure his happiness. Dominique, on the other hand, continues to feel nothing but resentment. Marcandier (the insurance company owner) and Dominique, both self-serving hypocrites who wish to profit from Frontignac Senior's eventual demise, conspire to bring about a decline in his health. Marcandier calls at Frontignac's home to deliver the latest installment of the annuity which is costing him so much. At this point, Frontignac, having consulted with his solicitor, proposes to Marcandier that, in order to "get [his] hands on some money, quickly," the latter return his capital investment to him, in exchange for Marcandier's being released from the obligations to pay Frontignac. Marcandier sees the advantage of accepting this offer, given that Frontignac has "an iron constitution" with the result that Marcandier is "carrying too much risk." Just as in the Verne story *Jédédias Jamet,* then, the greed and materialism of the bourgeoisie is mercilessly satirized throughout this comic play. Frontignac, on the other hand, is continuing to evolve over the course of the play, from a self-centred rogue into a more selfless, altruistic and loving uncle: reflecting on his deal with Marcandier, he muses "this is going to change my lifestyle somewhat, but what of it! Savinien is a good fellow!"

However, it is at this point in the play—just as Frontignac appears to have turned over a new leaf—that he receives an unwelcome reminder of the romantic indiscretions of his past. He is visited by Antonia Roquamor—pursued, as she rightly guesses, by her jealous, suspicious spouse who is, correctly, convinced that his wife has been having an illicit liaison with Frontignac. She begs him to give her back a letter she has recently sent him wherein she had added a romantic postscript which, if discovered by her husband, could lead to her downfall. While Frontignac pretends that he lovingly rereads her letter every day, the truth is that he has no idea where it is. When the jealous husband bursts into the apartment, Antonia pretends to have come to inspect it because it is, she maintains, available for rent. This seems to placate her husband for the moment; her ruse has succeeded.

In the meantime, Carbonnel changes his mind about allowing his niece to marry Savinien de Frontignac, and tells the young man's uncle that he will give his consent to the marriage on condition that the uncle "disentangles [himself] from his business arrangement with Marcandier" and takes out a life insurance policy instead, which will eventually allow Savinien to inherit. Frontignac, having already spoken to his solicitor, instantly sees the merit of this idea. He then begins to worry about his mortality and the idea of tempting fate by insuring his life, but Carbonnel (being doubly self-serving in that he is the owner of the life insurance company) assures him that "all those centenarians whose names you see published in the newspapers are clients of ours … I would even wager you that, back in the day, the late Methusaleh himself … there can hardly be any other way to explain his extraordinarily long life." Carbonnel forces Frontignac to undergo a medical examination prior to the signing of the new policy, which causes much anxiety to Frontignac, who is, however, overjoyed when told by Doctor Imbert that "you stand a strong chance of outliving us all." The scene in which Frontignac undergoes the medical examination is one of the comic highlights of the play: Frontignac himself is extremely anxious as to what the outcome of the doctor's tests will be, while Marcandier, who has asked to be allowed to be present while the doctor is examining Frontignac, is equally beside himself. It would, of course, be in Marcandier's interests for Frontignac to be diagnosed as being in poor health, so that the life insurance policy would be refused and he (Marcandier) could then retain the lump sum in question, but this turns out not to be the case.

Towards the end of the play, Frontignac, in perfect health, is presented with his life insurance policy, though it is almost nullified when Marcandier and Frontignac declare that they are about to fight a duel, which is narrowly averted by Carbonnel. In the final scene, Antonia has persuaded the young lovers not to elope to San Francisco; the couple returns in a guilty, confused state but they are, finally, overjoyed when given their blessing by Carbonnel and Frontignac Senior. It is a happy ending for all except the hapless Marcandier, who declares, just before the final curtain: "I am ruined!"

This play is one of contrasts: between the formerly cynical Frontignac and his unworldly nephew; between Madeleine, a virtuous young woman infused with the ideals of true romantic love and other female characters such as Antonia who are led into infidelity by Frontignac Senior; and between the initially unsympathetic Frontignac Senior and the changed man he becomes after meeting his nephew. Though Verne satirizes the self-serving behavior of several characters throughout this play, he ultimately allows the nobler sentiments of true love (platonic as well as romantic) to triumph over mercenary considerations. Similarly, in the second play to be considered here, *The Castles of California,* Verne ridicules the materialism and social climbing of the Parisian *petite bourgeoisie,* before illustrating once again that real, unselfish love—both of the romantic and familial kind—is the only value. So, as we shall now see from an analysis of the plot and themes of *The Castles of California,* both plays have similar themes.

At the outset of *The Castles of California,* Catherine, housemaid to the impoverished though socially-climbing Madame Dubourg (who has deluded herself into believing that her husband, on his way back from California, has become a millionaire), greets a visitor to the household, a young man called Henri Fremont, a travelling salesman and merchant who aspires to the hand in marriage of Madame Dubourg's daughter Henrietta. As with the characters of Savinien and Madeleine in *A Nephew from America,* Henri and Henrietta are deeply in love and quite unconcerned with material gain, unlike their parents and other characters encountered in the course of *The Castles of California.* Catherine assures the anxious suitor Henri that Henrietta's affection for him can be depended upon, ironically using the language of a speculator when she says to him that Henrietta's "friendship for you is rock-solid; it's a watertight investment." However, Catherine simultaneously acknowledges that the young lady's mother, Madame Dubourg, will be a likely obstacle to the course of true love, as her head has been turned by delusions of grandeur and wealth, and she seems to want her daughter to marry an aristocrat as opposed to the humble Henri. Madame Dubourg's husband had immigrated to California three years earlier for economic reasons, and he is now on his way back to Paris, having convinced his wife that he has become a millionaire through successful speculation, the streets of Sacramento, California having been "paved with gold." Both Henri and Catherine agree that this may be wishful thinking on Madame Dubourg's part and that her husband "has perhaps found nothing other than financial ruin, again just like so many others!" On the strength of her husband's apparent newfound wealth, Madame Dubourg has been running up huge debts through extravagant purchases on credit, buying such articles as fashionable hats and cashmere shawls. She is portrayed as somebody who is "trying to keep up with the Joneses," as she hopes to make her friend Madame Dubuisson jealous through her superior garments. She will thus, as Henri puts it, "need to have a millionaire as a son-in-law." In this regard, she is reminiscent of Carbonnel in *A Nephew from America,* as he, too, expects his niece to marry a man of fortune; however, Madame Dubourg, and many of the other characters in this second play, are depicted with much more exaggerated comic traits, making this vaudeville farce a typically burlesque comedy of its time. Catherine advises Henri not to give up hope and to be patient, as she suspects that Madame Dubourg's dreams of grandeur will probably come to naught.

Throughout the day on which the action of the play takes place, a succession of suppliers arrive at the Dubourg household to deliver expensive items ordered on credit by Madame Dubourg: a milliner, a dressmaker and a tapestry-maker among others. Henri realizes that she has run up much debt, and that it will be impossible for her to pay it, so he settles it with some of the creditors. In the meantime, Monsieur Dubourg arrives home from Sacramento, deliberately disguised as a poverty-stricken man, dressed in ragged clothing; he believes that he has become a millionaire but wishes to first play a trick on his family by pretending that he has come back destitute. At first, neither Catherine nor Madame Dubourg recognize him, and, comically, imagine him to be a thief; however, it is the Dubourg children who realize that this man is actually their father. Henrietta hopes that her father's indigence will make him realize that the love of a united family, and of a happy marriage, are the most important values in life; however, Monsieur Dubourg then declares that he is, after all, a millionaire, and that Henrietta will have to marry Alexis, a young man who has called to the house several times that day asking to see "Baron Dubourg"; and claims that he is a

Russian aristocrat. However, Catherine arrives back from an errand to declare that the bank run by the "House of Edwards" has been ruined—and Monsieur Dubourg realizes that he is, once again, destitute. Catherine exposes "Alexis" as her good-for-nothing nephew who immigrated to California some years previously, taking all her savings with him. However, the story ends happily; "Alexis" decides to marry Catherine's niece Clara with whom he has been in love for some years, while Henrietta and Henri also find the way clear for them to marry. The moral of the story, as iterated by several characters in the closing scene, is that the love of family and the values of hard work are the key to true happiness, while wealth is illusory. As Catherine sums it up in the final line of the play, "Faraway hills are not always the greenest." She also quotes the proverb which forms the play's subtitle: "A rolling stone/Father (*pierre/père*) gathers no moss."

Thus, the moral of both plays is similar. It is also worth noting that one of the novels which Jules Verne completed just a few years prior to his death, *The Hunt for the Meteor*, shares some of these fundamental themes. As with the two plays in this volume, *The Hunt for the Meteor* is a satirical, humorous work in which Verne deals with themes of human greed; in this case, the desire for the vast amounts of gold contained within a newly-discovered meteor which is found to be circling ever close to the Earth's surface. In the town of Whaston, Virginia, in the United States of the late nineteenth century, two rival amateur astronomers, Dr. Hudelson and Mr. Dean Forsyth, both have astronomical observatories built within their homes, and are constantly seeking to outdo each other in their celestial discoveries. When they simultaneously discover, through their respective telescopes, a previously unseen meteor in the skies above their home town, they both immediately report it to two separate professional observatories, and both receive acknowledgement. Each man is madly jealous of the other. The rivalry intensifies over the course of the novel, reaching such a degree of bitterness that it initially prevents the planned wedding of Forsyth's nephew, Francis Gordon, to Jenny, the elder daughter of Dr. Hudelson. This unfortunate halt of the wedding of the young couple comes despite the best efforts—including repeated admonitions—of Forsyth's redoubtable housekeeper Mitz and Dr. Hudelson's younger daughter, the feisty fifteen-year-old Loo. When it is discovered by the professional astronomers at the Boston observatory and other similar official institutions that the meteor—which un-

Frontispiece for *The Hunt for the Meteor*, showing the rival astronomers and their observatories.

der the attraction of the Earth's gravity is due to land somewhere on the Earth's surface in early August of that year—contains literally trillions of dollars worth of gold at its core, the various countries throughout the world in which the meteor is thought to have a chance of landing become embroiled in bitter, complex negotiations over how the gold should be distributed. Thus, human greed and pride is satirized mercilessly by Verne, both at the individual level of Forsyth and Hudelson and at the level of humankind generally; an international commission finds it impossible to reach a consensus, owing to the self-interest and avidity of all parties. As the expected date on which the meteor is due to hit the Earth draws ever nearer, it is estimated by astronomers that a particular region of Greenland is the most likely landing place. Thus do the official representatives of the various nations with a claim on a share of the gold—together with thousands of curious members of the public from all over the world—congregate in order to witness the momentous landing. Unsurprisingly, their numbers include Forsyth and Hudelson, each of whom still hopes to have the meteor named after him, and perhaps even to be munificently granted some small share of the gold contained therein. Their parochial, petty bickering has become increasingly overshadowed by the international political and economic rivalry which has ensued on a global scale. Thus do the two men gradually put aside their mutual resentment, becoming ever more united in their resentment of Greenland and Denmark's primary claim of the meteor. The denouement of *The Hunt for the Meteor* shows all of the human greed and resulting conflict to have been futile, as the meteor ultimately falls into the ocean, with the gold lost forever. The postponed wedding of Francis Gordon and Jenny Hudelson, initially prevented through familial in-fighting motivated by pride and financial gain, finally takes place. Verne heaps ridicule upon those who speculate for gold and on the vanity of human nature. As in *The Castles of California* and *A Nephew from America,* aspirations towards wealth are confounded, and love wins out.

One other notable similarity between this novel and the plays is found in the characters of the respective housekeepers: Catherine in *The Castles of California* and Mitz in *The Hunt for the Meteor.* Both Catherine and Mitz seek, in vain, to warn their employers against the futility of wealth and social status, and try to facilitate the course of true love. Both are feisty, humorous characters who are not afraid to speak their mind to their employers. In the end, each is found to have been dispens-

Housekeeper Mitz scolding Dean Forsyth in
The Hunt for the Meteor.

ing wise advice all along, and the outcome desired by both—a happy, if not wealthy, household—is achieved. Curiously, in Jules Verne's original draft of *The Hunt for the Meteor*, Mitz does not utter the sort of malapropisms regularly used by Catherine in *The Castles of California.* This appears in Michel Verne's reworking of the novel, where Mitz is made to utter many humorous puns and other misuses of the language of proverbs, such as "met dehors" for "météore."

Twenty-first century readers are now invited to enjoy these two comic plays from the pen of a young Jules Verne, translated for the first time into English, and which resonate so clearly with his novels.

The Castles of California

The Castles of California,
or A Rolling Stone Gathers No Moss

A play which provides entertainment for all the family; a one-act comedy based on a proverb.

CHARACTERS:

MONSIEUR DUBOURG, an architect, businessman and entrepreneur.

HENRI FREMONT, a travelling salesman and merchant.

ALEXIS.

MADAME DUBOURG.

HENRIETTE DUBOURG, Monsieur Dubourg's daughter.

MARGUERITE, PAUL, Monsieur Dubourg's children.

CATHERINE, the cook.

CLARA, Catherine's daughter.

A milliner, a dressmaker, a tapestry-maker, a water carrier.

The action of this play takes place in Paris, in 1852. The scene depicts the drawing room of a middle-class household, with evidence of both luxury and poverty. There is a door to the back and doors at the sides.

SCENE I.

HENRI, CATHERINE.

CATHERINE: So finally, it's you again, Monsieur Henri, after two months' absence? I thought you'd completely forgotten about us.

HENRI: Me, my dear Catherine! But I've never for one moment stopped thinking about you all.

CATHERINE: You mean you've never stopped thinking about Mademoiselle Henrietta.

HENRI: Especially about her, oh! Yes!

CATHERINE: That's a fine idea! Oh, I know what you're like: straight as a diet and with your hand on your heart, as the old proverb goes.

HENRI: (*Laughing.*) I see you haven't given up your old habit of reinventing traditional wisdom…

CATHERINE: You need to have a laugh every now and then … life isn't all a bed of roses. You must agree, though, that you seem to have taken the long way round!

HENRI: I had to undertake this last business trip in order to get promoted. Through dint of hard work, I've been successful! I've set up three new branches for my boss…; my salary has doubled … and …

CATHERINE: Bah! You know quite well that it isn't money that … You're here, and that's the principal thing: better late than never![1] As the old proverb … That

1. In the French source text, the housekeeper and cook, Catherine, utters several malapropisms throughout the course of this play, and is thus one of the most

must have made you two thousand crowns, all the same …

HENRI: Which doesn't include my share in the profits …

CATHERINE: Damnation! You could set up a home with somebody for less than that …

HENRI: Do you think that I shall be able to give Mademoiselle Henrietta …

CATHERINE: Oh, don't have any worries at all on that score …; her friendship for you is rock-solid; it's a watertight investment.

HENRI: Oh! Thank you, Catherine! … And her mother, Madame Dubourg?

CATHERINE: Ah! Well now, that's the fly in the ointment … Since your departure, there's been nothing but commotion and upheaval around here … I might as well tell you that the lady of the house has lost her mind.

HENRI: She has gone mad?

CATHERINE: Well, just about. When I entered into service in this household, as you will remember no doubt,

---

humorous characters in this piece, especially in the early scenes such as this one. Her frequent comic misuse of words tends to center on her misquoting of various French proverbs, including the proverb which forms the subtitle of this play (as we shall see towards the conclusion of the play, when the wordplay in question occurs). In this particular instance, her French utterance is "Mieux vaut lard que navet" (which literally translates into English as "Better bacon than turnip," and is a mispronunciation on her part of the actual French saying "Mieux vaut tard que jamais," which means "Better late than never"). The wordplay-derived humor here is based on French phonology, and is thus extremely challenging to convey, with equivalent effect, in target language English with its differing phonology. Therefore, in translating this comic utterance, it has been decided by the translator to explain the wordplay by means of this footnote.

Monsieur Dubourg had already been gone away for a long time; for I don't even know him, the poor dear man, despite my being like a sister to his wife!

HENRI: Yes; when he saw that the construction industry was coming to a standstill, he set sail for new horizons, just like so many others.

CATHERINE: And, just like so many others, he went off to seek his fortune in California …

HENRI: Where he has perhaps found nothing other than financial ruin, again just like so many others!

CATHERINE: That's how it will all end up, of course! In the meantime, he's come to the conclusion that all that glitters is indeed gold, and he even wrote to us after landing in California that the streets were paved with gold and that he was literally raking it in! When she heard all that, the lady of the house … well, her head started to spin like a weather vane … she dreams of nothing but velvet and diamonds … I've been wasting my breath trying to talk some sense into her, saying: "But, Madame, faraway hills look green! At least wait until Monsieur Dubourg gets back! Don't trust that Sacré-menthol place or whatever they call it." (There's a so-called Christian name for you, that can't be uttered without an oath!) "But, Madame, I too have a young rascal of a nephew in California," says I to her "a right little scamp who wanted to act the grown-up gentleman, and upped and left us while he was still in short pants and wet behind the ears …; the proof is that he carried away everything I owned with him, one hundred crowns which it had taken me ten years to earn … When he got there, he announced, just like the gentleman of this household, that he was going to send us hundreds and thousands of crowns!

And I leave you to guess whether they've started to arrive! … I haven't had any word from him for three years, except once when he again asked me for money, on the pretext that some savage had scalped him, which means that he'd taken off the skin from his skull! He must be a right-looking oddball these days! Me, send him money, like hell I will! If I ever come face-to-face with that fellow, ever again!" Well, that's what I was saying to the woman of the house … well! I might as well have been wasting my sweetness on the dessert [sic] air! Her Ladyship thinks she's a millionaire, and there you have it!

HENRI: I see … and will she need to have a millionaire as a son-in-law?

CATHERINE: I'm afraid it looks that way … at least until such time as she comes back down to earth.

HENRI: I shudder at the very thought …I know Monsieur and Madame Dubourg: he is a man of wit, but lacking in strength of character; she, a woman of some imagination, though lacking in sound judgement.

CATHERINE: I'd advise you to be patient: he who laughs last laughs loudest![2] It may not be long before they wake up to reality …There's something in the air today, it seems. I have no idea what's gotten into her Ladyship! There's some piece of news in the offing, I bet! She's got something up her sleeve; well, she's all hare-brained today, rushing hither and thither, making all sorts of grand preparations for something or other, as if she was about to give lodgings to the King of the Indies … She's ordered

2. In the French source text, Catherine intends to quote the proverb "Rira bien qui rira dernier" ("He who laughs last laughs longest"). What she actually utters is "Rira bien qui rira derrière," which literally translates as "He who laughs last laughs behind."

in all sorts of lavish luxuries, it's like a feast of Salbazar, if you don't mind! Well, I've got to dress up in a blue cloth, begging your pardon …

HENRI: Some rival, no doubt, an intended who has to be dazzled … Ah! Catherine, what should I do?

CATHERINE: Don't throw out the baby with the dishwater, I'm telling you …

HENRI: Well, as it happens, you're right; if Mademoiselle Henrietta loves me, there will be two of us against one.

CATHERINE: There will be three of us!

HENRI: My dear Catherine! You're helping me regain some of my courage … By the way, I'd completely forgotten to ask you for news of Henrietta's little brother and little sister, and of Mademoiselle Clara, your charming daughter!

CATHERINE: The children are well, thanks to their sister and me. Clara is still here and still the same. She, too, is dreaming about California, and she's been going round all the shops with Madame Dubourg … Would you believe that I just can't get that rogue of a nephew of mine out of her head! – "I love him just the way he is, truly I do" – huh! That's her answer for everything. She's just refused a match made in Heaven: a rubber-seat manufacturer … Oh! Youth! Well! Who's coming in now? This house is bedlam …

HENRI: (*To Catherine.*) Could it possibly be my rival in love?

CATHERINE: (*To Henri*). Our King of the Indies! Allow me to shut his beak for him.

SCENE II.

HENRI, CATHERINE, ALEXIS. (*The latter having the face and clothing of a most eccentric, dandified gentleman. A hooked moustache, windswept hair, a tie, waistcoat and gaudily-colored trousers. A short, yellow overcoat. He is wearing bracelet charms, rings on his fingers and a pince-nez in his eye.*)

CATHERINE: What larynx-like eyes![3]

ALEXIS: Sir … my good lady housemaid, may I speak to the gentleman Baron Dubourg, if you please …

CATHERINE: The gentleman Baron Dubourg! What on earth is all this about?

ALEXIS: A Parisian gentleman, who has gone into business as a pastime. Is this not his private townhouse?

CATHERINE: It's here, and it isn't at all over there …

ALEXIS: And so, it ***is*** here, then.

CATHERINE: He isn't here … he's absent on business concerning "ladies' choice."

ALEXIS: So, where shall I be able to find him?

CATHERINE: In Saint-Catch-a-Crown,[4] in California.

---

3. In this instance, Catherine says "Quels yeux de larynx" ("What larynx-like eyes"), when, presumably, she means to say "What sphinx-like eyes."

4. Catherine occasionally mispronounces the place name Sacramento, here saying, in the French original, "Saint-attrape-sot," which literally translates as "Saint-catch-an-idiot" or "Saint-catch-a-crown." In other instances throughout this play, she is seen to mispronounce it in other ways, e.g. "Sacre-menthol" is another English translation I have used to secure equivalent humorous effect.

Alexis et Henri (scène II). Dessin de M. Eugène Forest.

N.-B. Le spirituel dessinateur a fait ici deux malices d'un seul coup de crayon. En même temps que les deux jeunes premiers du Proverbe, il a représenté les modes d'aujourd'hui, bien portées et mal portées. Avis à nos lecteurs fashionables.

Alexis and Henry.

ALEXIS: (*Aside, keenly observing Catherine.*) That's very strange, that tone of voice is not at all unfamiliar to me. (*Aloud.*) He has gone to San Francisco! I thought that Monsieur Dubourg had returned.

CATHERINE: Do you wish to speak to Madame?

ALEXIS: No, thank you! (*Aside*). It is quite clear to me that I am not at the Baron's home. But where on earth have I heard that voice before? (*To Henri*). I beg your pardon, a thousandfold, Sir! (*He bows and leaves*).

SCENE III.

HENRI, CATHERINE.

HENRI: Who on earth can that character be?

CATHERINE: Some adventure-seeker or other, who got the wrong front door … Dubourg is a very common name.

HENRI: I hope so … for if it's a barony one is after …

CATHERINE: My God! I'm not vouching for anything. Still, there's no sign of Madame getting back here in any hurry.

HENRI: Still, I do wish to speak with her; I must know my fate!

SCENE IV.

HENRI, CATHERINE, a female milliner, followed by a female dressmaker, and a tapestry-maker. Comical faces.

THE MILLINER: (*A cardboard box in her hand.*) Madame Dubourg?

CATHERINE: You've come to the right place.

MILLINER: There's the hat which Madame has ordered. (*She takes an eccentric-looking hat out of the box.*)

CATHERINE: What was I telling you just now?

MILLINER: I shall call back this evening with the invoice. (*She exits.*)

CATHERINE: And there goes yet another one of them. That's what Madame has been up to since this morning.

HENRI: She must have got some news of her husband.

THE DRESSMAKER: Madame Dubourg?

CATHERINE: And there's a second; yet another one of them. You've got the right house.

DRESSMAKER: Here is Madame's dress. (*She unfolds a dazzling dress.*) May I see her?

CATHERINE: She's gone out.

DRESSMAKER: I'll call back this evening. (*She exits.*)

CATHERINE: With the invoice. The procession is starting, and we're still only at the front banner. Ah! There's the beadle.

A TAPESTRY-MAKER: Madame Dubourg?

CATHERINE: You're in the right place.

TAPESTRY-MAKER: I'm here to bring Madame some samples of wall hangings.

CATHERINE: Madame isn't here, and I know nothing about any of this.

TAPESTRY-MAKER: I'll come back in an hour. (*He exits.*)

CATHERINE: (*To Henri.*) Well, so you see what's been going on round here!

HENRI: But this is quite alarming! How can we save her from certain ruin?

CATHERINE: Ah! How indeed! The good God Himself will have to get involved, because if anyone tries to give her the slightest warning or piece of advice, she just flies off the handle like milky soup … Whatever you do, don't say anything to her face to vex her … You'd end up becoming her pet hate, and all would be finished. Better to pretend to be going along with her ideas.

HENRI: And push her into the abyss? Never! Even if her husband were to bring her back gold, I know what becomes of these suddenly-acquired fortunes. Have I not just this morning learnt that the House of Edwards, that great Sacramento bank, is about to suspend its payments? …

CATHERINE: Speak to me of a station in life such as yours. A bird in the land is worth three in the thrush …[5]

HENRI: No! I know what I've got to do. (*He writes a letter. Then, in an emotional tone of voice.*) Take this, Catherine, and if I am refused Henrietta's hand in marriage, if I am hunted away from here, and if poverty should enter this household in my place, you shall open this letter and give it to her whom I shall love forever!

SCENE V.

HENRI, CATHERINE, MADAME DUBOURG (*the latter entering in an aghast state*), then CLARA.

HENRI: Madame Dubourg!

5. In the French original, the malapropism uttered by Catherine is "Un bon chien vaut mieux que deux plus gros rats," which literally translates as "A good dog is worth more than two bigger rats."

CATHERINE: At last … And Clara? What have you done with her?

MADAME DUBOURG: I've left her at the East India Company.

CATHERINE: As security for some purchase?

MADAME DUBOURG: (*Not listening.*) Has my hat been delivered? Has my dress been brought? Has my Indian shawl arrived yet?

CATHERINE: Here's your hat; they'll be back later with the invoice…

MADAME DUBOURG: Very well. Next …? My velvet mother-of-pearl dress …twelve meters all round …

CATHERINE: There it is, your dress! The dressmaker will be back with the bill …

MADAME DUBOURG: That's good, that's good! … And my shawl?

HENRI: (*Greeting her.*) Madame!

MADAME DUBOURG: (*Noticing him.*) Ah! Good day, Monsieur Henri … And my shawl, my Indian shawl with a white background, pure Tibetan, with the brand name on it … But I can't see it anywhere.

CATHERINE: Neither can I. Perhaps it's still in Monsieur Dubourg's suitcases.

MADAME DUBOURG: My husband! (*Aside.*) Could she, by any chance, have found out that … (*Aloud.*) I say, Catherine, when that cashmere shawl is delivered, you are to say that I am not at home.

CATHERINE: And I won't accept delivery of it?

MADAME DUBOURG: Have you taken leave of your senses? On the contrary … By the way, Monsieur Henri, will you dine with us today?

HENRI: Thank you a thousand times, Madame; but …

MADAME DUBOURG: You accept! … A splendid dinner! Three full sittings … I don't yet know how many starters I shall have. I shall consult with Chevet on that matter. I want there to be three different soups! What do you think? Catherine?

CATHERINE: (*In a low aside to Henri.*) What! Well, what did I tell you?

HENRI: Madame Dubourg, listen to me, I beg you.

CATHERINE: (*In a low aside.*) Not just yet! Wait, and let me do the talking … (*Leading Madame Dubourg into a corner.*) Madame, you're about to find out that the suppliers aren't prepared to give you any more credit.

MADAME DUBOURG: Bah, what of it! One day more, and I shall pay them.

CATHERINE: Madame, they're quite serious about this and they aren't beating about the thrush! They won't give me anything else without cash in hand.

MADAME DUBOURG: How annoying! Bother! What must be done? I'll tell you what, Catherine, let's opt for simple things which you will lay out as ornately as possible … What is called, in polite society, the architecture of the dinner table …

CATHERINE: But … what on earth do you mean now?

MADAME DUBOURG: A large fish, a fine pork pie. You'll prepare the stuffing?

CATHERINE: But I've got nothing to stuff the inside, let alone anything to buy the outside!

MADAME DUBOURG: You are such a silly woman! I shall arrange it all with Chevet. Go to the kitchen, and when my cashmere shawl arrives, you shall accept delivery of it with all due honors …

CATHERINE: Ah! Good Jesus! Lord above! In Heaven's name!

(*Enter Clara, carrying a jewellery box in one hand, and in the other, a cardboard box containing cashmere.*)

MADAME DUBOURG: (*Springing towards the cardboard box, and unfurling the shawl.*) There it is! She has brought it herself, that dear child … Kiss me, and come here and let me try it on. (*She puts the shawl round her shoulders and admires it.*) How beautiful it is! Oh, yes, how beautiful it is! And how mad with jealousy it shall make Madame Dubuisson, who has only got a French one! Ah! But I was almost forgetting to show off the label. (*She refolds it and tries to hand it to Clara.*)

CATHERINE: Okay, just for once, Madame … This mad behaviour of yours, it's as contagious as whooping-cough.

CLARA: Try to have a little patience, mother, and my cousin shall bring me back one just like it …

CATHERINE: That cousin of yours is nothing but a flaming idiot, and I forbid you to defile his name.

CLARA: I love him just the way he is, truly I do, and that's all there is to it!

CATHERINE: (*To Henri.*) You can recognize the same old song!

CLARA: And I have my reasons for counting on him. (*She gives a knowing look to Madame Dubourg.*)

MADAME DUBOURG: (*In a low aside.*) Be quiet! My little pet.

CATHERINE: Come on, come with me to peel my carrots while we wait for the ones from Sacra-menthol! (*In a low voice, to Henri.*) And as for you, please try to talk some sense into Madame's brain, that's if she hasn't already made a vol-au-vent of it for her gala evening. As for me, I'm off to throw caution to the wind. (*She leads Clara offstage.*)

SCENE VI.

HENRI, MADAME DUBOURG.

MADAME DUBOURG: (*Distracted and busy dressing.*) You are staying, Monsieur Henri? Is there something you wish to speak to me about?

HENRI: Yes, Madame, and it's on a subject which isn't new. You know how much I love …

MADAME DUBOURG: This hat … (*She tries it on.*) It has such a lovely shape; it's from Laure's boutique! – Eighty francs, without the feathers!

HENRI: Mademoiselle Henrietta …

MADAME DUBOURG: Shall also have one, and I swear to you that she'll be able to walk along beside her mother!

HENRI: Indeed, I wished to ask you, Madame, whether Mademoiselle Henrietta has been transformed just like you in my absence; whether, just like you, she now bases her happiness on clothing and finery.

MADAME DUBOURG: (*Examining her dress.*) This dress comes from Pamela's boutique! How easily one can tell! … That artist has a talent for showing things off to their full effect! … What elegance, when compared with Madame Dubuisson's smocks!

HENRI: (*Sadly.*) For the last time, Madame, I have the honor of speaking to you about your daughter; just two months ago, she was an angel of modesty and simplicity, and you know what depth of sentiment her virtues, as well as her graces, had inspired

"PANNING," ON THE MOKELUMNE.

Panning for gold along the Mokelumne River, California.

within me; I had dared to aspire to her hand in marriage and, as you yourself admitted, she had been quite willing not to rebuff that hope of mine.

MADAME DUBOURG: (*Laughing.*) Ah! Your matrimonial plans! You are still thinking about those?

HENRI: (*Keenly.*) Might she have forgotten about them, Madame?

MADAME DUBOURG: My dear Henri, let us speak frankly; two months ago, Henrietta was the daughter of a poverty-stricken architect, and had the manners and habits becoming of that social position. She is now the heiress of a wealthy capitalist, a millionaire …

HENRI: A millionaire! Are you certain of that?

MADAME DUBOURG: Well, isn't her father coming back from California?

HENRI: Ah! Madame, so many people have gone out there poor, and have come back absolutely destitute!

MADAME DUBOURG: What? A land where one only has to bend down to pick up gold ingots! Where the destitute beg with golden begging bowls! Where people are so rich that a leg of lamb costs an ounce of gold! Do you mean to tell me that you think Monsieur Dubourg has been just folding his arms in that earthly paradise?

HENRI: You're only seeing the good side of everything, but what about the bad side, Madame! You choose to ignore the dreadful disasters of which California is the scene, the fires which break out each month, the daily struggles, the nightly murders. That gold which you imagine to be so easily obtained, it is gathered with a pickaxe in one hand and a rifle in the other; and for every settler who makes his fortune, there are a thousand who succumb to destitution and hunger.

MADAME DUBOURG: (*Ironically.*) So, do you hope that Monsieur Dubourg is one of those?

HENRI: Me, Madame! I pray that it may please God that your wishes will come true! But do remember that you can count on me, should Monsieur Dubourg fail in his speculations.

MADAME DUBOURG: He shall succeed! – He has succeeded! – I forbid you to say that my husband isn't a millionaire! … And hold on a moment, I want to prove to you that … Great God! What a racket! … What on earth is going on?

SCENE VII.

HENRI, MADAME DUBOURG, a water-carrier. (*The water-carrier aggressively and roughly pushes away Catherine and Clara, who are trying to block him from coming in, and he enters, slamming the door in both ladies' faces.*)

WATER-CARRIER: I'm coming in, by Jove!

MADAME DUBOURG: (*In a transport of joy.*) A delivery man! It's my casaquin![6] Is he delivering my casaquin?

6. A casaquin is a type of corset, current in Verne's time. The noun "casaquin" is a French word which has, here, been transferred, untranslated, into the English translation of this play, in order to preserve the cultural flavour of the text (but with the addition of this explanatory footnote). The original word used by

WATER-CARRIER: I'll be damned! I'm asking you for the last time, when are you going to pay me?

MADAME DUBOURG: I say! It isn't my casaquin! But who are you?

WATER-CARRIER: I'm the water carrier, upon my word! And you owe me no less than eighteen francs and fourteen centimes!

MADAME DUBOURG: Ah! I'd forgotten about that debt! Eh! My goodness! No need to get angry! (*Searching in her pockets.*) My purse … Where has my purse got to, then! … Could I have lost it? … But I had a considerable amount of money in it!

WATER CARRIER: Is this some kind of joke, this showy nonsense of yours? Give me my money or I'll smash up everything in this house! (*He knocks over Madame Dubourg's hat, which had been placed on the table.*)

MADAME DUBOURG: Stop! My hat! My hat from Laure's boutique! … And how bothersome it is that I don't have that purse … I'm sorry, Monsieur Henri … Ah! I have come over quite faint. (*She falls back into a chair, in a fit of hysterics.*)

HENRI: (*To the water-carrier.*) How much is owed to you?

WATER-CARRIER: Eighteen francs and fourteen centimes, by Jove!

HENRI: (*Taking out his wallet.*) There's twenty francs; keep the change, and just get out of here!

Verne in his source text was "casawech," which proved impossible to locate in any French-English dictionary or through online searches. Further research has come up with "casaquin" as the most plausible word in question, and for this information the translator is indebted to Oxford University Press lexicographer Dr. Susie Dent.

WATER-CARRIER: That's fine by me! Is that it, then? Good evening, all … By Jove! (*He exits.*)

HENRI: (*Aside.*) She invites me to a feast, and I end up lending her twenty francs! Will she learn her lesson from all this?

SCENE VIII.

HENRI, MADAME DUBOURG.

MADAME DUBOURG: (*Recovering her composure.*) At last! He's left … Thank you, my dear fellow, for getting rid of that awful brute.

HENRI: (*Bowing.*) Madame! I am only too happy …

MADAME DUBOURG: Oh! All those people shall pay me dearly for the distress they are causing me! And just so you don't think that I'm allowing myself to be deluded into believing falsehoods, listen to me, and keep what I am about to tell you strictly confidential. (*Reading from a letter.*) "My dear wife, the three-master *La Cérés* has just arrived in Nantes; it has brought me back to you, in good health. As soon as my business on board has been completed, I will take the train and I shall fall into your arms! Your husband, François Dubourg."

HENRI: Monsieur Dubourg? He's coming back?

MADAME DUBOURG: His letter came the day before yesterday; he could thus arrive here at any moment.

HENRI: Thus, Mademoiselle Henriette …

MADAME DUBOURG: My daughter now has an elevated standing in high society!

HENRI: (*Trembling.*) *Madame*, it now remains only for me to once again put my question to you, and I beg you to tell me the whole truth. Has Mademoiselle Henrietta adopted your ideas on riches and happiness?

MADAME DUBOURG: When you have made your fortune, my dear fellow, you will realize that one immediately accustoms oneself to it. (*Speaking in a serious tone.*) My daughter knows that she shall become, at the very least, a countess, one of these days! … It can already be seen that she was born to occupy that high rank; in a word, it can be acknowledged that she is worthy of her mother!

HENRI: (*Aside.*) Alas! She no longer loves me, then! … She is lost to me! I'm leaving, I can't take any more of this!

MADAME DUBOURG: (*Holding him back, and speaking in a protective tone.*) Well! Must we leave each other on such terms? Are you afraid of being friends with us now that we've become rich? Well, my dear Henri, we shall help you to make your way in the world!

HENRI: Please allow me to take my leave of you, Madame. (*Aside.*) I wouldn't have the strength to see Mademoiselle Henrietta again!

MADAME DUBOURG: Come, now! You know quite well that you are staying to have dinner with us! No more of this childish behaviour! We shall continue to see each other as friends; from now on, it's of no consequence, and …

SCENE IX.

HENRI, MADAME DUBOURG, HENRIETTA.

HENRI: (*Pretending to exit.*) Mademoiselle Henrietta! …

MADAME DUBOURG: (*Going towards her daughter.*) What! Henrietta, haven't you put on your glazed silk dress?

HENRIETTA: (*Running to Henri's side.*) Ah! Monsieur Henri, how pleased I am to see you again!

HENRI: (*Greeting her sadly.*) Mademoiselle …

MADAME DUBOURG: Well! Henrietta, will you please answer me? Why have you not put on your glazed dress?

HENRIETTA: What good would it do, Mother?

MADAME DUBOURG: But, my dear child, one has to make use of these beautiful things. You are rich and happy, aren't you?

HENRIETTA: (*Extending her hand to Henri.*) Oh, yes! Very happy!

HENRI: (*In a low aside.*) Is this a dream! … An illusion!

MADAME DUBOUG. (*Examining herself in the mirror.*) Look at my hat! I so enjoy wearing it, that I'm going to keep it at home.

HENRIETTA: (*To Henri.*) You aren't saying anything to me! You are sad upon your return! Are you no longer the same to me? … Have I changed in your eyes?

HENRI: (*In a low voice.*) I'm afraid of all this! … Does your heart not know that … you are a millionaire?

HENRIETTA: (*Seriously.*) What are you saying, Henri?

MADAME DUBOURG: (*Still in front of the mirror, and not hearing the young people.*) Do you see, Henrietta, look at how the shape of hats has become wider and more opened out. Madame Dubuisson is being ridiculous with all her comings and goings in the corridor! I quite like this new style of hat … And you?

HENRIETTA: Yes! It's very elegant. (*To Henri.*) So, you thought that my feelings for you would change once I became rich?

HENRI: (*Shyly.*) Mademoiselle … I'm sorry! Your good mother …

HENRIETTA: My poor mother is being deceived by her overactive imagination. I pray to God that her dreams will come true, for she would suffer too much from any disappointment.

HENRI: But what about you, Henrietta?

HENRIETTA: Me! I believe that poverty is quite conducive to happiness; and were Heaven to grant me these treasures which I desire so little, I would use them to create, somewhere, for myself, the humble nest we were hoping for … two months ago …

MADAME DUBOURG: (*Who has overheard her, and speaking in an aside.*) Mercy! What on earth is she saying?

HENRI: (*Rapturously.*) Oh! Mademoiselle Henrietta, I could give my whole life to hear such words and it would not be enough!

MADAME DUBOURG: (*In a firm tone of voice which brooks no disobedience.*) Henrietta, come here and help me to fold my cashmere shawl in the latest fashion.

HENRIETTA: Yes, Mother. (*She goes to help her mother.*)

HENRI: (*Aside.*) So, Madame Dubourg was mistaken! And to think that for one minute I could have imagined that …

MADAME DUBOURG: (*Placing the shawl on her shoulders.*) Not like that … the label can't be seen. In any case, I want to wear it long. My God! This is difficult! (*She folds and refolds the shawl.*)

HENRI: (*To Henrietta.*) But, Mademoiselle Henrietta, your mother is most anxious for you to have the benefit of all these splendid riches which your heart does not at all desire; she wishes to raise you to the heights demanded by your newly-found wealth!

HENRIETTA: What wealth?

HENRI: (*Aside.*) She doesn't know that her father has returned!

HENRIETTA: And even if our social standing was to change, why should our heart change? The heart is never impoverished.

MADAME DUBOURG: (*Aside.*) Oh, oh! I've been playing with fire. (*Coming forward and standing between them both.*) I am sorry, Monsieur Henri, to interrupt your conversation; but you seem to have already forgotten what I was saying to you only a moment ago. And as for you, Henrietta, you have done your father the insulting disservice of doubting him!

HENRIETTA: My father!

MADAME DUBOURG: Just think, then, that he is the very model of a financial speculator, and that a man like him must succeed in all his endeavours!

HENRIETTA: Eh! My dear mother, success cannot make him any happier, for happiness awaits him in our midst, and he has only to return; he has only to live alongside those whom he cherishes and who love him! A father who creates and shares his children's joy is a millionaire at his own fireside.

HENRI: (*Effusively.*) Oh! Thank you, Mademoiselle, once again, thank you!

MADAME DUBOURG: (*Severely.*) Mister Future Banker, you ought to know that people come back from California laden down with banknotes!

HENRI: And what if they do come back with banknotes, Madame!

HENRIETTA: (*Sadly.*) And what if they do come back, Mother!

MADAME DUBOURG: (*Aside.*) Most definitely, this young man cannot remain here. (*In a loud voice, self-consciously and awkwardly.*) *Monsieur* Henri, I am truly sorry, but … my gala dinner … cannot take place this evening … I must therefore beg you … to accept my sincerest apologies …

HENRI: She's throwing me out!

HENRIETTA: (*Aside.*) What does this all mean? I feel as though I'm about to burst into tears!

HENRI: I still thank you, Madame. (*He bows to her.*) Goodbye forever, Mademoiselle! (*Aside.*) I prefer this enforced taking of leave, which at least allows me some hope! (*Henrietta bows, sadly.*)

MADAME DUBOURG: I'll see you out, Monsieur Henri. (*Both exit.*)

SCENE X.

HENRIETTA (*Alone*).

HENRIETTA: What sadness is in my heart! My mother's words are causing me such pain, she is mistaken; my God! I derive so much pleasure from thinking about Henri, that all the treasures in the world couldn't make me any happier! When he returns home, my father will understand me! If only he could come back poor! Oh, but I mustn't think along those lines, my poor mother would be so much to be pitied! Well at least, there is one consolation remaining to me: this great dinner shall not be taking place, and will not swallow up, in an instant, the little bit of money I've earned.

SCENE XI .

HENRIETTA, CATHERINE. (*Holding a feather duster and a sweeping brush.*)

CATHERINE: Ah, there now! Still in tears?

HENRIETTA: It is you, my good, kind Catherine!

CATHERINE: Haven't you seen Monsieur Henri at all?

HENRIETTA: On the contrary, he has just left us a moment ago!

CATHERINE: Well then, for pity's sake, be joyful for all our sakes! It'll be of some help in relieving our worries … in this court of the King of Stupidity! Madame has sent me to dust the drawing room, and she's more intent than ever on holding this gala evening of hers!

HENRIETTA: (*Keenly.*) For what day?

CATHERINE: For this evening, Goddamn it!

HENRIETTA: But Mother has just told Henri that this dinner wouldn't be taking place.

CATHERINE: For him, it may very well not be taking place; but Madame has her own set of chatter-boxes and dinner plates lined up.

HENRIETTA: (*Weeping.*) Oh! My God! So it was, therefore, a notice to quit, a dismissal of Henri! I understand everything now!

CATHERINE: (*Aside.*) Okay … so I'm going to also have to upset her. (*Aloud.*) Come on now, my dear little Henrietta! Take courage, and be patient. Time is a great sealer [sic], come on now! Forgive my abruptness; but the thing is, the affronts are raining down heavily upon me just now, and it stirs me up to see money being thrown away, left, right and center …

HENRIETTA: (*Wiping her eyes.*) Here you are, Catherine, here are some pieces of needlework I made without my mother's knowledge. (*She hands her the pieces of embroidery.*) Try to sell them to pay off the most pressing debts.

CATHERINE: What an angel! What a blessing from the good God above! And to think that Madame is uncorking bottles of champagne, without any idea of all this!

HENRIETTA: We must respect these little whims and extravagances of my mother! I will work harder, my dear Catherine, and I shall pray for my father's safe return!

CATHERINE: Oh, he'll be back alright, your father will; but in what state, that's the question, as the old proverb says.

HENRIETTA: Somebody is coming! I'm getting out of here, for my eyes are all red from crying! (*She exits.*)

SCENE XII.

CATHERINE, ALEXIS.

ALEXIS: (*Entering from the rear.*) I've been assured that I have come to the right place. May I speak to Baron Dubourg, please?

CATHERINE: (*Aside.*) Not this odd character again! (*Aloud.*) He isn't here; he is in Sacre-menthol, as I've already told you …

ALEXIS: (*Aside, casting sidelong, surreptitious glances at Catherine.*) This is most odd! That voice isn't at all unfamiliar to me!

CATHERINE: (*Becoming angry.*) Well! Are you just going to stay planted there like an idiot …

ALEXIS: You don't know when he is due back?

CATHERINE: From Sacre-menthol? I do declare! It takes no less than six months to get back from that place …

ALEXIS: (*Aside, casting sidelong glances at her.*) That voice most decidedly makes me uneasy! (*He exits.*)

SCENE XIII.

CATHERINE. (*Alone.*)

CATHERINE: Now there's a fine specimen of a moustachioed fellow who likes to put on airs and graces! Now if only he was coming to bring some money; but I think he's coming instead to ask for some. (*She tidies the furniture.*) Ah! Now if only Madame had an ounce of sense in that head of hers, she would

Catherine (scène XIII). Dessin de M. Eugène Forest.

Catherine.

send Cupid's arrows flying in every direction; she'd marry her daughter off to that little young man, and we'd then only have the two nippers to whip into shape … But no, she has to bite off her nose to spite her face! Let's sweep the room then, since it has to be swept! … A bad tool which creates more dust than it gets rid of … Good! There's the leg of a chair about to go walkabout. (*She adjusts it as best she can, haphazardly.*) Mortgaging cashmere shawls on the millions from Sacre-menthol! I'd bet two coppers that her husband will come back. I bet he'll be as much use to us as the fifth wheel of a carrot! Well!

SCENE XIV.

CATHERINE, MONSIEUR DUBOURG. (*Monsieur Dubourg comes onstage dragging an old suitcase after him; he is dressed in an old, patched trousers, a sort of bizarre jacket and a wide-brimmed hat, which gives him the air of a Spanish bandit.*)

DUBOURG: Whew! A seat to rest my weary head! (*He sits down on the broken chair and falls flat on his back.*)

CATHERINE: Yet another intruder! What does this one want?

DUBOURG: I travel three thousand leagues only to fall onto a chair like this!

CATHERINE: (*Folding her arms.*) Look at this! So you've come to break all our furniture, have you, whoever you are?

DUBOURG: (*Still seated on the floor.*) And what furniture! … This is elegant enough for a millionaire!

CATHERINE: What are you looking for – charity? We shan't do anything for you.

DUBOURG: (*Sniggering.*) Madame has her poor to look after?

CATHERINE: Yes, my fine fellow! (*Aside.*) You can bet your bottom dollar that she has her poor to look after!

DUBOURG: (*Mocking her.*) Charity begins at home, doesn't it?

CATHERINE: (*Aside.*) What is he going on about? He has the head of a villain; what if he's a thief!

DUBOURG: (*Standing up and walking round the room with an air of self-importance.*) These old-fashioned things can't stay here! I'm going to have everything taken away!

CATHERINE: (*Aside.*) Have everything carried away? He's a thief! (*Aloud.*) So, do we have to call the police?

DUBOURG: Why, my good woman?

CATHERINE: His good woman!

DUBOURG: Well, you **did** call me your fine fellow!

CATHERINE: (*Shouting.*) Help! Thief! Thief!

DUBOURG: (*With a comically threatening gesture.*) You foolish woman!

CATHERINE: (*Yelling.*) Thief! Help! Murderer!

DUBOURG: (*Aside, laughing.*) Come on, this is going well! This is going well! (*Shouting with her.*) Help! Thief! Thief!

CATHERINE: (*On her knees.*) Ah! Monsieur Crook, spare my poor mistress! Have mercy, God in Heaven!

DUBOURG: (*Aside.*) Well! How easily an honest man can look like a bandit!

SCENE XV.

MONSIEUR DUBOURG, CATHERINE, MADAME DUBOURG.

MADAME DUBOURG: (*Entering from the left.*) What on earth is all this racket?

CATHERINE: Lord Jesus! It's some convict or other, Madame!

DUBOURG: (*Aside.*) There she is!

MADAME DUBOURG: (*Not recognizing her husband.*) Ah! My God! Word has already got out that we've become millionaires! They've come to loot our house!

DUBOURG: (*Greeting her majestically.*) Madame!

MADAME DUBOURG AND CATHERINE: (*Running round in every direction.*) Help! Police!

SCENE XVI.

MONSIEUR DUBOURG, CATHERINE, MADAME DUBOURG, MARGUERITE, PAUL, HENRIETTA. (*They run up from several different directions.*)

HENRIETTA: What's the matter with you? What's going on?

THE CHILDREN: Ah! Mother! Mother!

CATHERINE: (*Entreating for help.*) Mercy! Have mercy!

THE CHILDREN: (*With a shout of joy.*) Hey! Dad! But … it's Dad! (*They jump up and embrace him round his neck.*)

HENRIETTA: My father! (*She too embraces him in the same way as the children.*)

DUBOURG: Oh voice of nature! They've been the first to recognize me!

MADAME DUBOURG: Him! Him! Dubourg?

CATHERINE: That's him! The master of the house!

DUBOURG: (*Solemnly.*) It is I, in the flesh – and bones; and especially bones, as you can see …

MADAME DUBOURG: (*Flinging herself into his arms.*) Ah! My poor husband!

CATHERINE: (*Aside.*) So he's left all his millions at the foot of the stairs! (*Hugging and kissing—a scene of family happiness and reunion.*)

THE CHILDREN: Dad, have you brought us back golden toys?

MADAME DUBOURG: Alas! My friend, I'm all too afraid that I can guess what's going on here! … (*She sits down.*)

HENRIETTA: My poor mother! (*A moment's silence.*)

DUBOURG: Most decidedly, Meyerbeer is a great man. (*Singing.*)* And as for gold, it's nothing but a pipe-dream.

* Giacomo Meyerbeer (1791–1864) was a German composer who moved to Paris and became known for his melodramatic operas.

LES CHATEAUX EN CALIFORNIE, OU PIERRE QUI ROULE N'AMASSE PAS MOUSSE.

COMÉDIE-PROVERBE EN UN ACTE.

Le retour de M. Dubourg (scène XVI). Dessin de M. Gavarni.

The return of Mr. Dubourg.

MADAME DUBOURG: (*Aside.*) What a strange state of mind he's in! Could he have gone mad?

DUBOURG: What is that vile metal which vanishes into thin air so swiftly? It isn't worth all the work it takes to acquire it, nor the worries it causes in trying to hold onto it!

HENRIETTA: (*Affectionately.*) My dear father, you are undoubtedly very tired! Don't you wish to rest?

DUBOURG: (*Frivolously.*) Me, tired! And why on earth should I be tired? I've arrived with empty pockets, an empty stomach and an empty head! Never have I felt more light-headed and light all round before today! There was only one thing I was afraid of, and that was of being blown away by the wind!

CATHERINE: Would Sir care to have something to eat?

DUBOURG: So, my good woman, you're no longer afraid of me, then? Do I still look as if I've come to rob somebody?

CATHERINE: Oh, my crafty fellow, you don't at all look as if you're worth robbing, either!

DUBOURG: The enormous privilege of my social position! (*Addressing his wife.*) Come now, my dear wife, let us not be upsetting ourselves at all! I haven't come back empty-handed. I have brought with me …

MADAME DUBOURG: (*Keenly.*) What is it, then?

DUBOURG: Certain eminently philosophical convictions on the instability of human, material things, on the grandeur and decadence of the Romans in general and of settlers in particular. If only you knew how little wealth matters, when one wants for nothing!—Paul, give me a handkerchief. (*Paul obeys.*) Well, riches matter even less when one wants for everything!

HENRIETTA: (*Sadly.*) If my poor mother wasn't crying so much, I would be as philosophical as my father.

DUBOURG: Wealth doesn't bring happiness, but it certainly contributes to it, as some millionaire whose name escapes me once said, someone who was obviously biased and prejudiced; as for me, I consider that, on the contrary, it is happiness which brings riches! People who are content with having very little are envied by all, so just imagine the well-being of those who are content with having nothing at all! – Housemaid, please see to lunch! – I'm ravenous – I feel as though I'm emerging from a long spell of solitary confinement with only bread and water to drink on the *Medusa* raft! Ah! How rich is one, when one can feast on one's reflections! A steak now and again doesn't do any harm. Housemaid, put potatoes round the meat; but as for philosophy; let it be rare, at least – that is the true nourishment of humankind! *Vanitas va* (*with an gesture towards Catherine*) *nitatum.*[7]

CATHERINE: (*Aside.*) Why is he calling me *nitatum?*

MADAME DUBOURG: (*Dismayed.*) Goodbye forever to my dreams! What's going to become of me?

DUBOURG: (*Aside.*) Has the lesson been completely learnt?

THE CHILDREN: Mother, you mustn't cry, can't you see that we're kissing you!

HENRIETTA: (*Consoling both her parents.*) My poor mother, my good father, where does happiness lie, if not in our joyous reunion after such a long absence? Does it count for nothing to be reunited with one's whole

7. "Vanitas" is the Latin word for foolishness, futility or empty pride; in sum, for Catherine, Verne is suggesting "Vanity of vanities."

family, and not to have to miss or long for anybody's fond kisses? Just look at how we're holding you tight in our arms! Look at Paul and Marguerite who can't understand why you're so distressed just when their father has returned home! Family: now that is true wealth. Look at how rich you both are!

DUBOURG: (*Kissing her effusively.*) What an excellent girl; always the same!

HENRIETTA: We will all work hard and will give you the affluence that financial speculations have denied you.

PAUL: I'm able to write—that's a start!

MARGUERITE: And as for me, I'm able to read big letters!

CATHERINE: And as for me, I'm able to cook boiled beef with vegetables, and I shall never leave you!

HENRIETTA: (*Speaking in a low voice to Catherine.*) Can you let Henri know what's going on?

CATHERINE: (*In a low voice.*) Come on now, it won't be long till he finds out. Just a moment ago, he was still outside underneath the windows. (*Aside, taking out from her pocket the letter which Henri has given her.*) Ah, here's a thing, I've just thought of it! This letter he left with me, for her … the moment has come to give it to her – it's now or never. (*In a low voice, to Henrietta.*) Hold on to this, Mademoiselle, while we wait for the young man. (*She exits.*)

HENRIETTA: (*Quickly reading it.*) A note from Henri! Am I seeing things? Oh! What a noble heart! But no, never! Now it's impossible! He mustn't come here now! Catherine! – Oh my God, she's gone!

DUBOURG: I say, my little children, allow me to speak to your mother. (*To Clara.*) And as for you, Mademoiselle, bring me a hot meal, quick as you like! (*All exit, except Dubourg and his wife.*)

SCENE XVII.

MONSIEUR DUBOURG, MADAME DUBOURG. (*They gaze at each other initially, without speaking.*)

MADAME DUBOURG: (*Aside.*) What a return he's made, and what a *tete-a-tete* we're having! And all my purchases! All my debts! But this is not just poverty—this is bankruptcy!

DUBOURG: (*With a very casual air.*) Well, my dear friend, and how is all our household management going? Have you managed to save some money while I've been away?

MADAME DUBOURG: Save … what?

DUBOURG: Not even any debts? So then, the position is clear! Nothing in our hands, nothing in our pockets! What have you been up to, then, over the past three years? You have dreamed some fine dreams, haven't you? You've only been unhappy for half the time, a year and a half!

MADAME DUBOURG: (*Aside.*) What a carefree, happy-go-lucky attitude! I don't recognize him any longer!

DUBOURG: My dear, we must hold on to our dreams, now more than ever. Above all, you must not despair; let's just take life one day at a time, as it comes, and take wealth … as it doesn't come! … Henrietta is a very accomplished young woman! That will serve us well.

MADAME DUBOURG: I have made a fine lady of our daughter; don't expect any assistance from her.

DUBOURG: (*Aside.*) That isn't the impression I got! (*Aloud.*) Well, let's just sit tight. We'll be well-off some day, thanks to some inheritance or other! Don't we have any elderly relative in their eighties? No! So, we don't have a penny to our name? But that's even better! All we'll have to count on is our future climbing of the social ladder!

MADAME DUBOURG: (*Dejectedly.*) Wait! Don't speak like that, you'll be the death of me!

DUBOURG: What! Can you not simply sweep over these petty obstacles? Are you afraid of destitution? Poverty; I'm not talking about that; it's a congenital defect! But destitution, that is the touchstone of all rich souls!

MADAME DUBOURG: Oh! This is all too much for me! I can't take any more of this fortune-seeking! But what did you get up to in that accursed country?

DUBOURG: I did all sorts of different jobs in which—just as here in Paris—I encountered a horrifying amount of competition. I unloaded merchandise from ships, carried heavy loads, ran errands in the city; Lady Luck smiled on me for three months; I used to look after cattle; that's quite a well-paid job. As for collecting gold, there was no point in even dreaming of it unless you were already a millionaire and could thus purchase lucrative investments, have essential tools made up, pay workers' wages each day, pay the never-ending legal costs of the perpetual court cases which you lose on a daily basis; not to mention all the acts of hatred, revenge, fires, thefts, attacks, looting, which are all accounted for in the liabilities column! I thus had to work with my bare hands, earn my bread through the sweat of my brow, and consider myself extraordinarily privileged whenever I saw some poet sweeping the streets or some senior statesman polishing boots. Go figure, then, whether—now that I'm back in France, and in spite of hunger and ragged clothes—I don't have a right to be happy!

MADAME DUBOURG: (*Sharply and excitedly.*) But don't you already hear our creditors yelling at the door?

DUBOURG: Our creditors?

MADAME DUBOURG: Alas! The seizure of our household possessions is the new mistress round here; but I won't just sit around waiting for it to happen! These cashmere shawls, these dresses, I'm going to send them all back to the shopkeepers. (*Wringing her hands.*) Oh! What a triumph this will be for Madame Dubuisson! (*She goes to fold the shawl.*)

DUBOURG: (*Stopping her.*) Just a moment, Madame Dubourg: you'll cause me to lose my credit!

MADAME DUBOURG: But how are we going to pay these suppliers?

DUBOURG: (*Majestically.*) Do I not have my signature? A highly-trusted signature, I do declare, and which comes from California!

MADAME DUBOURG: And once the due date for payment of our creditors comes round, your signature will be forced to go back to California, I suppose?

DUBOURG: But no! We shall earnestly await these creditors.

MADAME DUBOURG: And you think they're just going to go away the way they came?

DUBOURG: (*Solemnly.*) As a general rule: any creditor who comes in through the door always goes out through the window! Won't all our staff be here?

MADAME DUBOURG: Oh! My God! There can no longer be any room for doubt: hardship has caused him to lose his faculties!

DUBOURG: You still hesitate, you doubting Thomas of a woman, you! So you think my trip to California has been all for nothing? Not at all! I am equal to all social positions and to all the exigencies of domestic life! I shall be, all at once, my own lackey, coach driver, groom, chambermaid, cook, company, coach, horses; and, through my cheerfulness, my carefree attitude and my nerve, I shall get the better of the most monied aristocrats of this fine country we call France! So, go and see if dinner is ready, and if my asparagus and fowl has been suitably prepared!

MADAME DUBOURG: He is positively insane. Let us go, I can't take any more of this. (*She exits stage left, raising her hands to the heavens.*)

SCENE XVIII.

DUBOURG. (*Alone.*)

DUBOURG: (*With a huge roar of laughter.*) Ah! Ah! Ah! … The poor woman! … Perhaps I've overdone things just a little bit! So, she did the right thing in going out; my secret was about to escape from my lips, and my planned surprise announcement would have been nothing but a fiasco! Ruined? Me, ruined? When I've come back here, rich beyond my wildest dreams; when this wallet contains a million, to be counted this very evening! Ah! Lady Luck, as hostile as she had been up to then, finally reached out her hand to me while I was over there! Yes indeed, Lady Luck, I may well call it by that name; for I abandoned myself to the most insane financial speculations, the most adventurous business dealings. (*Rejoicing.*) And my streak of good luck hasn't run out just yet, I can feel it in the air! Oh! Back here, I'm going to capitalize on my fortune, and how! I shall triple it, quintuple it, until I can no longer estimate its amount! … So you see, my dear wife, you will be pleased with me! And as for you, my dear Henrietta, in a week's time, you'll be calling yourself the Princess of … Ah! The very man! There he is!

SCENE XIX.

DUBOURG, ALEXIS.

ALEXIS: (*Going through the same formalities as on the two previous occasions.*) Baron Dubourg, please?

DUBOURG: Ah! It's that dear prince …

ALEXIS: (*Failing to recognize him.*) I'm looking for Baron Dubourg?

DUBOURG: (*Bowing.*) I am he, in person. Will Your Lordship allow me to go to freshen up a little?

ALEXIS: (*Stepping back and peering at him.*) You, Dubourg! Ah! Well, I never! And what's the meaning of this complete transformation?

DUBOURG: A surprise, dear Prince, a whim, a study of social conventions! … I've just arrived this very moment, and I've presented myself to my family as financially ruined …

ALEXIS: (*Sharply.*) Between ourselves, you aren't really ruined, though, are you?

DUBOURG: (*Laughing.*) That would appear rather difficult to me! It would defy all the laws of fate. (*He takes out his wallet.*) My millions are right here.

ALEXIS: Allow me to shake their hand. (*He grasps the wallet tightly in both hands.*) So you stayed in Nantes for a few days?

DUBOURG: Of course; I wasn't as free as you, my dear Salsificoff. On board the *Ceres,* where we met, you were travelling like a prince, returning from America as wealthy as when you'd first gone there …

ALEXIS: Indeed; I was travelling the ocean for pleasure!

DUBOURG: But as for me, I had some profitable business dealings to see to in Nantes …Ah! The thing is, I was never cradled and wrapped up in the swaddling clothes of inherited wealth! Unlike you, Your Lordship, who was born just as you are today …

ALEXIS: Me? I can't even remember ever having been a child! It feels to me as though I never came into the world, but that the world, rather, came to me.

It seems that I have always had this keen eye, this aristocratic bearing, this face which is regularly … (*He pirouettes.*)

DUBOURG: Who are you telling? As soon as I first laid eyes on you, at twenty-five years of age, I exclaimed to myself: Now, there is a prince!

ALEXIS: But you yourself, Baron, you exude a certain air of good breeding …

DUBOURG: Well yes, in fact, it is claimed that I come from a very ancient lineage. (*Aside.*) I'm descended from Adam and Eve … on the women's side!

ALEXIS: (*Casually.*) You see, we other great Lords, we have some sort of *je ne sais quoi* which sets us apart at first sight! Do you know, my friends all declare that I've issued directly from Catherine the Great of Russia, herself, and that I have a thousand peasants to eat each day?

DUBOURG: A thousand peasants, no less! My word! Now that would be a way of making lots of gold! Those peasants could probably be opened up … Well anyway, Your Lordship, when I have the honor of having you as my son-in-law, we will set about becoming billionaires! … Money is everything! Honor, esteem, virtue! It is money which is canonized by high society! … Is five million not a great Saint?

ALEXIS: (*Laughing.*) A very tidy sum! A very tidy sum indeed! And when shall your daughter have the honor of being introduced to me?

DUBOURG: In just a moment, Prince. But first, she must learn the truth, and be made aware of my newly-acquired fortune.

ALEXIS: Without a doubt; I wish to be esteemed by her for what I truly am … Have you made quite certain that her heart is unattached?

DUBOURG: That goes without saying …

ALEXIS: Thus, her heart will belong completely to me?

DUBOURG: The heart is the capital of that limited partnership we call marriage; as soon as you buy all the shares in that limited company, you become the sole manager of it.

ALEXIS: You have remarkable strength of character, Baron; you philosophically consider that money brings happiness.

DUBOURG: Money, and the means of using it!

ALEXIS: (*Becoming confused.*) By the way, how come poor people aren't happy? Because they don't have any money; if they did have money, they wouldn't be poor, and not being poor … they would have money … Do you understand what I'm getting at?

DUBOURG: Admirably so!

ALEXIS: My dear father-in-law, I was forgetting something; you will have a few changes to make round here.

DUBOURG: I'm going to buy a manor, horses, coaches!

ALEXIS: You must also get yourself a new set of flunkeys! Get yourself people of distinguished livery … I'll have you know that I've called to this house several times already.

DUBOURG: (*Bowing.*) Your Lordship …

ALEXIS: And that I was uncivilly received by some sort of cook … (*Aside.*) The one whose voice …

DUBOURG: Her name is Catherine, I do believe, and comes from Auxerre in Burgundy.

ALEXIS: (*Aside.*) Catherine! Auxerre! … Damnation! I knew I recognized that voice! It's indeed my aunt!

DUBOURG: I shall ring for her this instant, and banish her from this household, in your presence.

ALEXIS: (*Holding him back, terror-stricken.*) In my presence! No, there's no point, it wouldn't be proper … The only thing I desire is not to run into her here ever again … Ah! I insist on that, I must say! My weakness is that I must absolutely insist upon that … It's a question of nerves …

DUBOURG: In that case, I'll send her on an errand while you're here, and when she gets back, I'll definitively dismiss her.

ALEXIS: (*Aside, breathing a sigh of relief.*) That's a great idea. (*Aloud.*) You will thus have done things according to etiquette … Ah! I can't wait to see the future Princess Salsificoff!

DUBOURG: There's somebody at the door! (*He goes to the door at the rear of the stage.*) It's my wife! … Your Lordship, please step into my study; we'll reappear as soon as I've completely stripped myself of this disguise.

(*They exit stage right, exchanging all manner of polite remarks and pleasantries.*)

SCENE XX.

MADAME DUBOURG, HENRI. (*Entering from the rear.*)

HENRI: As soon as I learnt of the misfortune which has befallen you, Madame, I decided to put all I possess at your disposal.

MADAME DUBOURG: (*Fanning herself.*) Ah! Kind sir, what a terrible thing it is to be broke! … Ah! I have suffered a blow from which I shall never recover!

HENRI: You must have a little courage and strength! Have people not been known to survive the most hopeless of situations?

MADAME DUBOURG: Our situation is not just a hopeless one, it's an absolutely lost cause …

HENRI: (*Insisting on his point.*) Allow me to correct your mistake and to work for you, Madame; for I happen to have faith in the future! Allow me to put you in a position whereby you can dream of tomorrow without worrying about today; and most of all, allow me to console that poor Monsieur Dubourg.

MADAME DUBOURG: Monsieur Dubourg! He's quite well able to console himself, I'm telling you! … What really finishes me off is precisely his lack of concern! … How can he take such horrendous misfortune so cheerfully! Oh! Men! Will we ever get used to no longer wearing lace and cashmere … especially when we've never even worn them … and were so close to doing so!

HENRI: But, Madame, answer me, if you please! … Time is of the essence, the least delay could prove fatal for you … Madame, accept what I offer! For the sake of your children ….

MADAME DUBOURG: Truly, Sir, I don't know … (*She hesitates.*)

HENRI: Oh! Thank you, you've made me truly happy, and now I shall run to … (*He makes to leave but is stopped in his tracks.*)

SCENE XXI.

MADAME DUBOURG, HENRI, HENRIETTA.

HENRIETTA: (*Appearing at the door to the rear.*) Stop! It's impossible, Monsieur Henri!

HENRI: Mademoiselle … you have just heard ….

HENRIETTA: No; but Catherine gave me this letter which you had written to me.

HENRI: Catherine … actually ….

HENRIETTA: Read it, Mother.

MADAME DUBOURG: "Mademoiselle, I find myself obliged to leave you and travel far away from you, and if my sad forebodings should come to pass, I wish to be sure that, for a while at least, poverty shall not weigh down upon you. Allow me then to lay at your feet, along with this bond of security, all that which I possess …" (*She drops the letter.*) Ah! That excellent young man!

HENRI: (*Keenly, standing up and offering the bond.*) Well! Madame, Mademoiselle …

HENRIETTA: (*In a dignified manner.*) Monsieur Henri, we are ruined; my greatest happiness would lie in recognizing your admirable sacrifice and devoting my whole life to making you happy; and if my father had brought us back any riches, my mother would say to you: Here is my daughter's hand in marriage! And I would feel the deepest joy in hearing her say it.

HENRI: Mademoiselle …

HENRIETTA: But I can't allow you to marry into a disastrous situation beyond repair; I can't make you responsible for a whole family with no resources and ho hope!

HENRI: (*Warmly.*) So, won't you trust to my courage and to my heart?

HENRIETTA: I shall never resign myself to burdening the man I love with my misfortune …

HENRI: (*Running to her side.*) Henrietta, in the name of God!

HENRIETTA: (*In a serious tone.*) It is impossible! (*She rejects the bond one final time.*) Goodbye …

SCENE XXII.

MADAME DUBOURG, HENRI, HENRIETTA, PAUL, MARGUERITE, CLARA. (*They come onstage from the rear.*)

THE CHILDREN: Hey! Look! That's our good friend! (*They run to Henri's side; he kisses them sadly.*)

CLARA: (*Alarmed.*) Madame! Mademoiselle! There's a dressmaker, a milliner, a tapestry-maker and a shawl merchant, all kicking up one hell of a fuss and demanding to see you. My mother has gone to deliver a letter from Monsieur Dubourg … I couldn't stop them from getting in …

MADAME DUBOURG: (*Aside.*) It's reached crisis point! … (*Aloud, impatient.*) Very well! … Ask them to wait … I'm going to … I …

CLARA: (*In a low voice.*) They say they're not going to leave until they're paid.

HENRIETTA: My God! My God! …

HENRI: Allow me to take care of this, Madame! Goodbye for the present, Mademoiselle!

HENRIETTA: Henri! I forbid you to …

HENRI: And ***I*** refuse to obey you! … (*He exits hastily, followed by Clara.*)

SCENE XXIII.

MADAME DUBOURG, HENRIETTA, PAUL, MARGUERITE, then CLARA. (*While Madame Dubourg and Henrietta look at each other in consternation, the children run about the room, touching everything and, finally, at the front of the stage, they open their father's old suitcase.*)

HENRIETTA: (*Drying her eyes.*) Mother, my poor father was absolutely drained with tiredness … Is his lunch ready, at least?

Henriette et Clara (scène XIII). « Des diamants, mademoiselle ». Dessin de M. Tony Johannot.

Henrietta and Clara; "Diamonds, miss."

MADAME DUBOURG: (*Distraught.*) I don't know … I …

HENRIETTA: (*Aside.*) Oh! I can't bear this, I'm suffering so! What does Henri plan to do?

MADAME DUBOURG: We must summon Catherine and find out …

HENRIETTA: You're forgetting that Catherine has gone out. (*Calling aloud.*) Clara! Ah! I do declare, I will see to my father's meal myself … I'll have to get used to this from now on … (*Speaking forcefully and vigorously.*) And you shall see that, with a little orderliness and hard work, we shall pull ourselves out of the abyss into which we have fallen! …

MADAME DUBOURG: Alas! May God hear you!

PAUL: (*Stopping Henrietta as she walks.*) Oh! What a lovely thing this is! Look, Henrietta, do you see?

MARGUERITE. Mother just look at this! (*They are removing different objects from the suitcase.*)

MADAME DUBOURG: (*Starting with surprise.*) A cashmere scarf!

HENRIETTA: A jewellery case!

CLARA: (*Who has just run back to them.*) Diamonds, Mademoiselle! An entire wardrobe of the finest clothes!

MADAME DUBOURG: Lace!

HENRIETTA: Good God! I'm shaking ! … Could it be that …

MADAME DUBOURG: (*Wild, beside herself.*) My daughter … I understand … your father … wanted to … Wealth has returned to us … oh! I'm losing my mind! … I've gone mad! … Ah! (*She wildly kisses Henrietta.*)

HENRIETTA: (*In a sharp, urgent tone.*) Clara! Run and stop … and inform Monsieur Henri … (*Clara exits.*)

SCENE XXIV.

MADAME DUBOURG, HENRIETTA, PAUL, MARGUERITE, DUBOURG, ALEXIS. (*Dubourg – now completely transformed from head to toe – and Alexis enter from the rear.*)

DUBOURG: (*To his wife.*) Can you forgive me for putting you through such an ordeal?

MADAME DUBOURG: (*With a cry of delight.*) We're rich! Ah! I shall die of happiness!

DUBOURG: (*Kissing them.*) My wife! My dearly-loved Henrietta! My children! Yes, we are rich, rich to the tune of millions!

HENRIETTA: Oh! Why does that word pierce my very heart?

ALEXIS: (*Scrutinizing Henrietta.*) Not bad! Not bad!

DUBOURG: (*To his wife.*) Here you are, my dear friend, wrap this Indian cashmere shawl round you! … Here, my Henrietta, embellish your charming forehead with these fineries! … My children, help yourselves to the treasures in this magical suitcase; when nothing remains, there shall be yet more!

THE CHILDREN: Thank you, dear Daddy! Thank you, thank you! (*They leap to wrap their arms round his neck.*)

MADAME DUBOURG: (*Attiring herself.*) How beautiful this all is! How magnificent this all is! Madame Dubuisson has been outshone! How could I have ever doubted your genius; ah! My friend, forgive me! All that is now missing from my happiness is your forgiveness!

HENRIETTA: Our happiness! Alas! Is everybody going to share in that happiness?

DUBOURG: I grant you a plenary indulgence. But first of all, my dear wife, allow me to introduce a son-in-law to you, and to you, my dear Henrietta, allow me to introduce to you—a husband.

ALEXIS: (*Greeting and scrutinizing her.*) Madame, Mademoiselle … (*Aside.*) Not bad! Not bad!

M. Dubourg transformé (scène XXIV). « Puisez dans cette valise. » Dessin de M. Tony Johannot.

Dubourg transformed: "Help yourselves to the treasures in this magical suitcase."

DUBOURG: (*Solemnly.*) His Lordship Prince Alexis Salsificoff, who is descended from the great Empress Catherine of Russia, and a member of the old Russian aristocracy, who has been especially distinguished with honors by His Majesty Nicholas.

MADAME DUBOURG: (*Becoming increasingly frenzied.*) A Russian aristocrat! My daughter shall be a Russian aristocrat! At this stage, my head is spinning! You are marrying into our family, Your Lordship? God! How good He is! Give me your hand, my son-in-law!

HENRIETTA: (*Overcome.*) Oh! How little memory is in my mother's heart!

DUBOURG: His Lordship, as you can see, is not the least precious of all that I've brought back from California! …

ALEXIS: (*Striking a proud pose.*) Yes, Madame, I am … delighted … to make … your acquaintance. During our return journey, the Baron Dubourg spoke to me at length about his social standing and his daughter: both suit me very well!

MADAME DUBOURG: May the Heavens be blessed! You will bring furs to us, Monsieur Russian Prince! … I adore fur! I must have a muff made of authentic sable fur. Madame Dubuisson's one is fake fur! Don't you see, Henrietta? I'll have talma lined for you with ermine fur. In the meantime, my friend, we shall celebrate your return in fitting style. I knew quite well that you would return triumphant, and I had everything prepared to greet you triumphantly! … I shall invite the whole city to dinner! … Ah! You shall be one of our guests, Madame Dubuisson! Madame Dubuisson! … His Lordship the Russian Prince of Salsificoff! …

ALEXIS: Madame, I am more and more flattered … to make … your acquaintance.

MADAME DUBOURG: (*Calling, aloud*) Catherine! Where's Catherine?

ALEXIS: (*Aside.*) Ah! No, by Jove!

DUBOURG: Catherine has gone to run an errand, but I shall dismiss her upon her return: that class of servant is no longer fitting for people of our high rank. Do you know that, in San Francisco, I was served by unemployed bankers, who weren't too proud to climb up on the back of my coaches? (*Speaking *with increasing exaltation, his excitement reaching its height.*) Oh! The thing is that I was all-powerful in that land where money brings total power. I felt, over there, that riches were becoming my slaves; my most outlandish speculations proved successful; I did business in clothes, food, housing, the breathing of miners; I bought enormous goldmines, from which I extracted credit and esteem; I captured the rain which fell on those burning plots of land, and the wind which carried ships to the Old Continent! Yes, I was the very embodiment of speculation, and I have come to practice my profession in a vaster and more productive domain; I want to transport the ground of San Francisco to Paris, to rescue gold-diggers from the perils of their journeys, make the Sacramento flow on the bed of the Seine; in a word, I'm going to buy the mountains of California in bulk, bring them back to France, and dig them for gold in the very heart of the capital! The whole of Europe will buy shares from me, and the Emperor Nicholas shall genuflect before me to get his hands on some of them; isn't that right, Monsieur Salsificoff?

MADAME DUBOURG: Ah! My friend! Kiss me! Again! Again! Kiss me, my son-in-law! How wonderful it is to have a Russian aristocrat here in the flesh! Don't you know what we're going to do? Tomorrow, we shall reserve the grandest stall in the Opera House, and we shall all appear there together in our Sunday best at the performance of *The Wandering Jew.* That will be our entry into high society! (*Throughout all of this scene, Henrietta has remained absorbed in her thoughts, as though she were having a bad dream.*)

SCENE XXV.

MADAME DUBOURG, HENRIETTA, PAUL, MARGUERITE, DUBOURG, ALEXIS, HENRI.

HENRI: (*Entering from the rear.*) Madame Dubourg, you no longer have anything to fear; here are your various bills which I trust you will pardon me for having settled for you.

MADAME DUBOURG: (*Heedlessly.*) What? What's all this about?

DUBOURG: What does this young gentleman want?

ALEXIS: (*Peering.*) Where has this gentleman come from?

HENRIETTA: (*Pluckily.*) This is Monsieur Henri Frémont, my fiancé, Father!

DUBOURG: What is the meaning of all this, Madame Dubourg?

HENRI: Monsieur Dubourg! What a transformation you have undergone! Oh! Allow me to …

DUBOURG: Enough, Sir. You have dared to aspire to my daughter's hand in marriage?

HENRI: (*Addressing Madame Dubourg.*) Madame …

MADAME DUBOURG: (*Embarrassed.*) My God, Sir, our position, wealth … a Russian prince … and then the Emperor Nicholas …

DUBOURG: Sir, please accept my thanks for the interest which you have shown in my family, for I believe I understand your devotion, and I shall fulfill my obligations to you this very evening. But, before

I returned, I had already promised my daughter's hand in marriage to another; you will thus understand how truly sorry we are … and also, that we're now millionaires …

ALEXIS: And it is I who am Prince Alexis Salsificoff, descended, according to my friends, from …

HENRIETTA: (*Falling into a chair.*) Oh! Father, you shall be the death of me!

HENRI: Sir, will you not take pity on an angel who is dying, and who—were it not for your ambition—would have found happiness in my own humble fortune!

DUBOURG: My daughter shall find consolation, Sir, in having the whole of California as her dowry. Any further insistence on your part would be out of place … Forgive me, Your Highness, for this preposterous incident.

ALEXIS: My forgiveness is granted!

HENRIETTA: Help me, Mother! Mother! Please!

MADAME DUBOURG: We are millionaires, daughter!

HENRI: (*Forcefully.*) Ah! Be on your guard, Monsieur and Madame Dubourg! Happiness is neither lined with silver nor sewn with gold, and that fortune which has come back from California turns upon a fickle wheel …

DUBOURG: Again, Sir, may I remind you that enough is enough! I have already had the honor of telling you that …

SCENE XXVI .

MADAME DUBOURG, HENRIETTA, PAUL, MARGUERITE, DUBOURG, ALEXIS, HENRI, CATHERINE, CLARA.

CATHERINE: (*Making an abrupt entrance from the rear of the stage.*) Ah! What misfortune! Ah! What good fortune! Ah! What misfortune!

ALEXIS: (*Horrified, in an aside.*) It's my aunt! (*Turning round and encountering Clara.*) It's my cousin! I'm caught between a rock and a hard place! … Let's try to beat a hasty retreat! … (*From now until the close of this scene, he tries to make his exit, but without managing to do so.*)

DUBOURG: So what is it now?

CATHERINE: That scrap of a letter you gave me …

DUBOURG: Indeed, I was informing my banker that he would have to draw on my bills.

CATHERINE: Yes! But, wake up everyone: the firm's been shut down!

DUBOURG: (*Stupefied.*) Shut down! The House of Edward!

HENRI: Heavens above! The House of Edward! It's just suspended its payment; it's more than a business going to the wall, it's a case of fraudulent bankruptcy! (*Dubourg falls, crushed at the news.*)

HENRIETTA: Father!

MADAME DUBOURG: Are we ruined again?

DUBOURG: Completely and irredeemably ruined! All my savings were in that bank, and the collapse of this bank will sweep away every other bank in America in its tide.

CATHERINE: Something new seems to happen every minute!

HENRI: (*After a silence.*) Mademoiselle Henrietta, our opportunity to marry has returned to us.

HENRIETTA: Indeed, yes! Father, will you allow your daughter to restore your happiness, by dint of hard work and affection?

DUBOURG: (*To Alexis.*) My Lord Salsificof, you are our last remaining hope!

ALEXIS: I am truly sorry, sir … to have made … your acquaintance. (*Aside.*) Let's try to beat a hasty retreat!

CLARA: (*Observing him carefully.*) Oh, my God! But don't I know that face from somewhere?

CATHERINE: (*Also recognizing him.*) It seems to me that I recognize that face, it's coming back to me like a bad penny.

ALEXIS: I am too honored … truly … but … (*Aside.*) Let's try to beat a hasty retreat!

CHILDREN: Monsieur Russian Prince, don't go away; you shall not go away! You promised us cake! (*They push him into a seat, leap onto his knees, start to pull at his beard and hair, with such force that they end up with a wig in their hands.*)

CATHERINE: (*With a shout.*) Mercy! It's my nephew! My nephew, who was scalped by the Zottentots!

ALEXIS: I've been caught rotten!

CLARA: (*Running to his side.*) My cousin! My dear cousin!

MONSIEUR DUBOURG,
MADAME DUBOURG
AND HENRIETTA: Her nephew! Her cousin!

HENRI: (*Pointing to the cook.*) Ah! Aha! So that's Catherine the Great, from whom His Highness is descended!

CATHERINE: I've got you at last, you worthless good-for-nothing! And you dare to pretend that you're a member of the nobility, no less!

ALEXIS: (*Confused.*) It isn't I … It is this gentleman here … who was calling me a prince …

DUBOURG: (*Similarly confused.*) And it is this gentleman here … who was calling me a baron …

CATHERINE: Yes, the devil finds work for idle hands; opportunity is seized by thieves, and birds of a feather flock together, as the old proverb says; but I'm sure that you're a beggar like Job, and that you don't even have my hundred ecus to return to me?

ALEXIS: Aunt … destinies and tides are ever-changing.

HENRI: Come now, Monsieur Dubourg! You have had the sort of dream a child has! You must now wake up as a grown man … You have mistaken shadows for real bodies and waxwork dummies for Russian princes … Twice poor and twice rich, all in the space of one day, you know what the castles of California are worth … Nothing has been lost, since you still have your reason, your family …

CATHERINE: (*Who has gone to get a casket in a corner of the room, with some crafty intention in mind.*) And what about this casket that you had left with Madame before you set off for California … I think it must conceal some nice little nest egg … From little acorns, big trees grow …

DUBOURG: (*Taking the casket.*) This casket? But I can't remember any more …

MADAME DUBOURG: What if it was some sort of treasure! …

DUBOURG: (*Opening the casket and removing therefrom a compass, a setsquare, a sounding lead, etc.*) The tools of my trade as an architect! (*Speaking with force and conviction, and with the air of a man who has finally been brought back to reality.*) Yes, it is indeed a treasure! The sort of treasure which braves reversals of fortune and bankruptcies! Intelligence, patience and hard work! (*Pressing the tools to his heart.*) I'm going back to my old profession, and I shall never give it up, ever again! Now that's true riches for you!

HENRIETTA: (*Flinging herself into his arms.*) Oh! Thank you! Thank you, Father!

DUBOURG: Your hand, Henrietta; and yours, Henri! (*He joins their hands together. Henri gives his hand to Madame Dubourg, and they form a happy family group.*)

HENRI: And there is true, solid happiness!

MADAME DUBOURG: (*Weeping, in an aside.*) At least I've still got my cashmere shawl for the wedding.

CATHERINE: And what about you, Clara, what do you think of your cousin now that he's penniless … and without any hair?

CLARA: (*Giving her hand to Alexis.*) I still love him, just as he is!

CATHERINE: So then, Alexis de Salsificoff, now that everybody is overjoyed, come and see whether there's any joy in beef stew. – And let's remember that faraway hills are not always the greenest. (*Looking at Dubourg.*) And that *a rolling Father gathers no moss.*[8]

THE END

8. In this final malapropism of the play, the subtitle "A rolling stone gathers no moss" is referred to: Catherine erroneously utters "A rolling father gathers no moss." The wordplay succeeds in the original French owing to the phonetic similarity between "pierre" (stone) and "père" (father). I have translated Catherine's malapropism literally, as she is, importantly to the theme of this play, referring to the father's (Dubourg) fruitless prospecting for gold in California and his return from his travels; in addition, the wordplay itself, as intended by Verne, is thus explained in this final footnote.

A Nephew from America

A Nephew From America, or The Two Frontignacs

A comedy in three acts

Performed for the first time on the stage of the Théâtre Cluny on 17th April, 1873.

CHARACTERS

ROQUAMOR, a wealthy Parisian gentleman and property investor.

ANTONIA, his wife.

DE FRONTIGNAC, STANISLAS, a Parisian gentleman of apparent means.

DE FRONTIGNAC, SAVINIEN, nephew of Stanislas.

DOMINIQUE, Stanislas' valet.

CARBONNEL, manager of a life insurance company.

MADELEINE, niece of Carbonnel.

MARCANDIER, an insurance salesman.

EVELINA, Marcandier's wife.

IMBERT, a physician.

Two GUESTS at Roquamor's soirée.

A SERVANT at the soirée.

ACT ONE

At Roquamor's home. A small living room.

SCENE I

MARCANDIER, IMBERT, A NUMBER OF GUESTS, and then ROQUAMOR.

A lively scene depicting a rather wealthy, upper middle-class ball; the doors to the rear of the stage are obstructed by guests who are getting crushed, rushing into each other and jostling each other; their backs are turned to the audience and they are looking in towards the room in which the dancing is being held. The sound of an orchestra playing can be heard.

FIRST GUEST: What a crowd!

SECOND GUEST: They've already had to break the glass of the windows!

FIRST GUEST: And no other refreshments to speak of!

SECOND GUEST: Are you acquainted at all with Monsieur Roquamor, the master of the house and host of this gathering?

FIRST GUEST: No! It was a friend who brought me here, as a matter of fact.

SECOND GUEST: Me too. All I know … is that his wife is a blonde … rather stunning …

FIRST GUEST: She isn't bad, I'll grant you that, but she does rather lack fullness of figure; personally, I tend to prefer ladies who are rather more on the buxom side … Oh! How bothersome! Just look at the state my hat has ended up in.

MARCANDIER: (*Coming on stage, accompanied by Imbert, and hearing these last words uttered by the first guest.*) As a general rule, remember this: when you go to a ball, remember to bring along an ***old*** hat!

IMBERT: (*Looking at Marcandier's brand new hat.*) Though it would appear that there are sometimes exceptions allowed to that rule.

MARCANDIER: (*A little embarrassed.*) What? Ah! Yes … well, let me tell you … I was simply unable to lay my hand on my own older hat.

IMBERT: Ah! … How fortunate for us to have found this little living room; at least here one can breathe.

MARCANDIER: The fact is that, if somebody could only cast a chill over this assembly, as it were …

IMBERT: What a remarkable idea of Monsieur Roquamor to give a ball! In the three years since he left Paris, nobody knows him anymore.

MARCANDIER: I would imagine that the idea was that of the wife rather than the husband. (*They sit down.*)

IMBERT: (*Noticing Roquamor.*) Sssh! Keep it down! Here he comes.

MARCANDIER: (*In a very loud voice, ostentatiously.*) Delightful party! Delightful party, indeed!

ROQUAMOR: (*Entering stage right and greeting them.*) Doctor … Monsieur Marcandier …

IMBERT: You've heard, no doubt, all the bad things we've just been saying about your party?

ROQUAMOR: Yes indeed … it ***is*** proving to be rather a success, isn't it? … The only thing that's annoying me is that, apart from yourselves, I don't know a single person at my own ball!

MARCANDIER: Well, what do you expect? You've been away for six months now in Marseille because of all these great property deals of yours. Upon your return, Madame Roquamor has the most fortunate and timely idea of giving a ball in order to enable you to renew your acquaintance with Parisian high society … Nothing could be simpler.

IMBERT: You must be delighted to see Madame Roquamor being so highly complimented, flattered and surrounded by so many admirers …

MARCANDIER: (*In a low voice.*) Will you be quiet, for God's sake! He's a madly jealous husband! …

ROQUAMOR: Yes indeed, come to think of it, now that you ***should*** happen to mention my good lady wife, will you just look at her and that crowd of little rascals who are toadying, skipping, fluttering and yapping all around her … Wait a minute! At the moment, she's dancing a polka with some sort of conceited, smug idiot whom I don't even know … and who's putting on all sorts of simpering airs and graces with her! My God … what a long polka this is … No … allow me … (*He gets up and tries to force his way through the crowd, towards the door to the rear.*)

FIRST GUEST: (*To Roquamor.*) I say, my good man, there's no need to push! A little decorum is in order.

SECOND GUEST: I presume you don't expect that you'll be able to simply pass right through our bodies?

ROQUAMOR: The thing is … I should have liked to …

FIRST GUEST: After the polka, sir.

ROQUAMOR: My sincere apologies, gentlemen; I shall wait. (*He goes back down towards the front of the stage.*) Most definitely, this fact of not being known to anybody is proving to be most tiresome.

MARCANDIER: Well, well! Are you not joining the dancers?

ROQUAMOR: Not unless I send for four men and a lance corporal to help me push my way through ***that*** crowd!

FIRST GUEST: (*Speaking to the second.*) Ah! Here is Madame Roquamor. What shoulders! What a waist!

SECOND GUEST: Not enough fullness of figure.

FIRST GUEST: It's all the same to me! She's quite something as far as I'm concerned, that woman! …

ROQUAMOR: Ah! But steady on now …

MARCANDIER: (*Restraining him.*) Calm down! Calm down! My dear fellow!

ROQUAMOR: Do you really imagine that this is a pleasant experience for me? I throw a party, I drive myself to the brink of financial ruin buying candles, punch, and ice creams and hiring wind instruments, and yet nobody so much as greets me or bids me the time of day; nobody pays any attention to me whatsoever. And what's more, people are treating me harshly, shouting abuse at me, jostling me about … Ah! Don't get me started! If this happens once more … I'm stifling in here! (*A servant enters, carrying a plate full of ice creams.*) Ah! Refreshments at last!

SERVANT: I beg your pardon, Sir, but it's ladies first, if you don't mind. (*The guests all rush towards the platter being held by the servant, which is instantly emptied of all its content.*) Gentlemen, gentlemen, please …

ROQUAMOR: Oh!

MARCANDIER: (*Peacefully enjoying an ice cream.*) Delicious! Excellent!

ROQUAMOR: All I've been able to get so far, at my own party, is a glass of barley water … all over my dinner jacket, that is …

FIRST GUEST: Well, that's how the cookie crumbles … I say, what a mess!

SECOND GUEST: (*Drinking a glass of punch.*) Go on out of that! It's all worth it … Good heavens! What on earth have they put into this punch?

ROQUAMOR: (*Furious.*) Indeed, my good Sir!

MARCANDIER: (*Holding him back and taking him by the arm.*) Stay calm! Good God! You give a ball, it causes you some annoyance, but do you think I'm enjoying myself or something? One has to be philosophical about such things, my good man; you'll have spent several hundred-franc notes, you will have been jostled, insulted, vilified, and your wife will have been courted by countless suitors; as for us, we'll have spent the entire evening yawning or losing our money playing gin rummy. Eh! By Jove, yet why complain? It would have been just as easy for you not to invite us, as for us not to reply to your invitation.

ROQUAMOR: My God, don't get me started! (*He gets up and walks back upstage, again trying to force a passage through the crowd.*)

FIRST GUEST: Ah! My good man, it's not you again, surely? Honestly, one just doesn't know what sort of people are being invited to these evenings any more! They'll let anybody in to gatherings like this, these days!

SECOND GUEST: Such improper, uncivilized behaviour!

ROQUAMOR: Just imagine, I have no choice but to go out into the corridors in order to get back into my own home! (*He goes out by a small door on the left of the stage.*)

FIRST GUEST: That perfectly uncouth man simply doesn't care about the social niceties!

SECOND GUEST: Oh, I daresay he's probably just some casual domestic who's been hired for the evening.

SCENE II

MARCANDIER, IMBERT, VARIOUS GUESTS; CARBONNEL and MADELEINE, *who enter stage right. – The latter two are walking along arm in arm.*

CARBONNEL: We're a little late getting here, it seems, but I do hope, my dear niece, that this little ball shall amuse and distract you, and that you will thus adopt a somewhat gayer countenance by the end of the evening.

MADELEINE: (*Looking round*) Perhaps he isn't here! (*In a louder voice*) A ball at which I know absolutely nobody …

CARBONNEL: With the exception of Madame Roquamor. I hardly know many more people than you do … But let's go look for the master of the house himself … (*Marcandier who is walking along with Imbert, meets with Carbonnel; the latter salutes him.*) That is he, no doubt. (*In a loud voice.*) Sir, it is indeed an honor for me to make your acquaintance. (*Marcandier displays an astonished reaction but returns his greeting. To Madeleine.*) It appears that I was mistaken. (*Greeting Imbert.*) I say! My good Doctor! Good evening, Doctor! How do you do?

IMBERT: (*Laughing.*) Not bad, and your good self? (*They shake hands.*) Did you take me to be the master of the house?

CARBONNEL: (*Pointing to Marcandier.*) You mean to tell me that that gentleman isn't the host of this evening, either?

IMBERT: (*Introducing him.*) I'd like you to meet Monsieur Marcandier, one of our most successful and prominent businessmen …

CARBONNEL: Delighted to meet you, Sir! An absolute pleasure, indeed!

IMBERT: (*Introducing him.*) And this is Monsieur Carbonnel, manager of the life insurance company ***The Lutetian***.

MARCANDIER: Delighted to meet you, Sir! Delighted!

CARBONNEL: A customer of mine, perhaps?

MARCANDIER: Yes indeed.

BOTH: Delighted to meet you Sir; absolutely delighted.

CARBONNEL: Do you know where we might be able to bid good evening to the master of the house, by any chance?

IMBERT: Monsieur Roquamor? He'll be in the grand drawing room, no doubt!

MARCANDIER: That must be where he is.

MADELEINE: (*Aside.*) And Savinien too, I truly hope so! He gave me his solemn promise that he would come here to be introduced!

CARBONNEL: Come, my dear niece. (*He takes her by the arm.*)

MARCANDIER and CARBONNEL: (*Putting on the same simpering show of airs and graces as earlier.*) Delighted to make your acquaintance, my fine fellow, absolutely delighted! (*Carbonnel and Madeleine exit the stage. The crowd has, little by little, divided and dispersed, and the guests have moved, some towards the left of the stage, others to the right.)*

SCENE III

MARCANDIER, IMBERT.

MARCANDIER: He's a charming fellow indeed, but I would rather like to take my leave at this stage.

IMBERT: Why did you come in the first place?

MARCANDIER: It's easy for you to talk; you're a bachelor, Doctor, but when one is under the yoke of female subjugation … Or perhaps just go and ask Monsieur Roquamor what I'm talking about.

IMBERT: And indeed, as we're on that very subject, isn't that your good wife, Madame Marcandier, that I see over there?

MARCANDIER: (*Looking over in the direction signalled.*) It is indeed she, in person … She's waltzing with Frontignac.

IMBERT: The handsome, distinguished, illustrious Frontignac.

MARCANDIER: (*Excitedly.*) You know him?

IMBERT: Only by reputation. The boldest and most unashamed pleasure seeker in Parisian high society; forever young, forever beavering away socially, in spite of the fact that the last time he saw forty-five was on a front door! The darned fellow must have an iron constitution to be able to withstand the sort of lifestyle he leads.

MARCANDIER: Yes indeed, it's impossible to find the slightest flaw in him.

IMBERT: What? You seem bothered by that.

MARCANDIER: Me; bothered? Not in the slightest, I can assure you. I'm well aware that there are others who, if they were in my shoes …

IMBERT: In your shoes? What are you talking about?

MARCANDIER: What, indeed; this very fellow we speak of is costing me twenty thousand francs a year and not a centime less.

IMBERT: What on earth are you talking about, man?

MARCANDIER: Oh, it's an idiotic story, I can assure you. If you can believe this, let me tell you that, just ten years ago, the self-same Frontignac was nothing but skin and bone, and was constantly coughing his guts out … To put it in a nutshell, he was falling away visibly, before my very eyes; he had swallowed up half his fortune and all he had left were barely three hundred thousand francs; a pretty packet, I grant you that, but one which, at the legally applicable rates, would have earned him nothing more than fifteen thousand in annuities. And in his case, fifteen thousand of private income was very little when it came to satisfying his luxurious lifestyle and appetite for pleasure; well, it so happened that there came along a good man, or should I say, a foolish one, who reasoned to himself in the following manner: Who will end up getting this fortune? Frontignac is unattached, alone, single, he has neither children nor heirs …

IMBERT: I see where you're going with this … Eh! By Jove, *I* ***myself*** can end up getting my hands on that fortune; so the worthy fellow reasoned.

MARCANDIER: I will give him ten per cent of his money, given the sorry state of his stomach, but if I actually end up having to pay him that for even one year, I'll be out of luck.

IMBERT: An excellent business arrangement, indeed …

MARCANDIER: Excellent stock, if you will. Six months later, his cough had disappeared and his stomach was as good as new. When you look at him today, what you see is a former sufferer of tuberculosis who has been cured by over-indulgence …

IMBERT: (*Laughing.*) Ha! Ha! Ha! And what of the worthy fellow who had gotten the idea of this business deal?

MARCANDIER: It was I! Good grief, and as that joke has been going on for no fewer than ten years now …

IMBERT: So let's just say that, if your friend were to fall into a hole, you wouldn't exactly be rushing over to pull him out of it…

MARCANDIER: My principles …

IMBERT: Prevent you from …

MARCANDIER: It isn't that. But, as you have just learnt, my life is insured and, as the holder of a life insurance policy, I am not allowed to risk my life in any way, as that would amount to defrauding the company.

IMBERT: You know, when all is said and done, it's all the same to me. Good evening …

MARCANDIER: Are you leaving so soon?

IMBERT: Well, I don't have any wife to bring back home, now do I?

MARCANDIER: Wait. Here comes Frontignac, walking in our direction with Madame Marcandier and Madame Roquamor in tow … Examine him, and let me have your opinion … Sometimes, these people who are built as though they were as strong as an ox …

IMBERT: Some other time. (*He exits the stage. The music stops. The dancers flock into the living room.*)

SCENE IV

MARCANDIER, FRONTIGNAC, ANTONIA, EVELINA, MADELEINE, CARBONNEL, ROQUAMOR.

FRONTIGNAC: (*Extremely over-attentive towards the ladies.*) There is no other than you, my dear lady, who could possibly throw such a wonderful party … One can no longer breathe, I do declare, one can no longer breathe … It's all positively delightful.

ROQUAMOR: (*In a low aside, to Marcandier.*) Who on earth is that fellow?

MARCANDIER: A fellow who's blessed with the nine lives of a cat, I can assure you. (*The ladies have sat down. Frontignac hovers round them.*)

FRONTIGNAC: I give you my word of honor! You think that I'm exaggerating … Before coming here this evening, I'd spent a few minutes at the ball being given by the Marchioness of Fumeterre; I'd devoted a quarter of an hour to the gala evening at Outremont and had had a quick look in at the society ball given by the Princess of La Rochetendron. Well! The noble faubourg, the Faubourg Saint-Honoré, are all left in the ha'penny corner, are quite outstripped … a fairy queen … you are a fairy queen! Where did you acquire that art, so rare nowadays, of being so kind, attentive, pleasant, friendly and gracious towards everyone? Words fail me. I am quite simply at a loss for words.

ROQUAMOR: (*Aside.*) That's what he calls being at a loss for words!

ANTONIA: Monsieur de Frontignac gives us credit for our efforts, as though they had been a success.

EVELINA: Monsieur de Frontignac happily sacrifices the divinities of yore at the feet of the divinities of today.

FRONTIGNAC: What do you mean, Madame?

EVELINA: (*In a low voice.*) You understand me, Stanislas?

CARBONNEL: Always the same!

FRONTIGNAC: Well if it isn't dear old Carbonnel! (*He shakes his hand.*) You'll never change me, I'm the same as when as I was an infant being weaned at my nurse's breast!

MARCANDIER: (*Aside.*) For the last forty-five years.

ANTONIA: (*To Madeleine.*) It seems to me, Mademoiselle, that you haven't yet had any dance … and yet there's no shortage of dance partners …

ROQUAMOR: (*Aside.*) It's floor space that there's a shortage of.

MADELEINE: Excuse me, Madame. (*Aside.*) And yet he had given me his solemn promise that he would be here this evening …

FRONTIGNAC: Can this be true? Well, in that case, if Mademoiselle would be willing to grant me the first waltz, I can guarantee that she'll enjoy herself.

MADELEINE: No thank you, Sir, I don't waltz …

FRONTIGNAC: That is such cruelty, Mademoiselle. (*He passes over to Antonia.*) You know, I was just saying to Madame Marcandier, Madame, that she ought to follow your example and give us one of these intoxicatingly delightful *soirées* …

MARCANDIER: Never! Monsieur de Frontignac can go and get drunk somewhere else. And what's more, we don't have the space to entertain in our home. Madame Roquamor, on the other hand …

ANTONIA: Ah! My good Sir, you are now reminding me of one of my causes of sorrow.

FRONTIGNAC: (*In a tone of regret.*) A cause of sorrow! There is something causing you sorrow?

ROQUAMOR: (*Aside.*) Is that any business of his? Is he going to start crying next?

ANTONIA: Yes! It's this apartment … we're going to have to vacate it; the owner is increasing the rent by a thousand crowns, and my husband, who's a positive tyrant …

FRONTIGNAC: Oh! Husbands! Husbands! What a species!

ANTONIA: (*Swiftly, introducing Roquamor.*) Monsieur Roquamor …

FRONTIGNAC: Ah! Sir, I'm delighted to make your acquaintance …

ROQUAMOR: (*Very stiffly.*) What?

FRONTIGNAC: I've been hoping for so long to finally have the honor of being introduced to you … I had heard Madame Roquamor speak of you in such flattering terms … such a witty, distinguished gentleman …

ROQUAMOR: (*Turning his back on him.*) Hmm!

MARCANDIER: (*Aside.*) Perhaps they'll end up devouring each other some day … Let's not rule out that possibility or give up on that hope!

CARBONNEL: Forever young, forever passionate, that Frontignac … you wouldn't think him to be even thirty years of age …

FRONTIGNAC: And if you did, he'd deny it. One doesn't age until one is good and ready … It was children who invented old age so as to be able to put their parents in a nursing home.

ANTONIA: Charming!

MARCANDIER: (*Aside.*) The truth of the matter is that he's in ruddy good health; he's healthy enough to make the hairs stand up on your head.

FRONTIGNAC: And to whom do I owe this eternal youth with which I'm blessed, this perpetual flowering of mine, with each new arrival of Spring? It is to women, my dear ladies, to none other than your good selves. For instance, this morning, I felt a little unwell, somewhat under the weather and lacking in energy. This evening, I'm cured, radically cured. And what did it take in order to effect this incredible cure? A society ball, nothing more nor less than a ball, that is to say, the sight of all of this ravishing sartorial finery, of all these naked shoulders (*In a lower voice, to Marcandier*) … these treasures which are so thinly veiled as to force more than one husband to venture out into polite society in order to truly appreciate his wife as she deserves. Isn't that so, Monsieur Marcandier?

MARCANDIER: Huh? What?

CARBONNEL: Well then, my dear fellow, since women are, for you, such wonderful doctors, how come you don't get married?

ANTONIA: Indeed.

MARCANDIER: (*Aside.*) Him! Get married! That's all I need!

FRONTIGNAC: I am a man of modern tastes, Madame, and window shopping suffices for me. I'm happy with just usufruct, as they say in legal circles.

ROQUAMOR: What …!

CARBONNEL: All the same, to establish a family for yourself, heirs …

FRONTIGNAC: Estates to be inherited, always! Heirs? Never! If I had had a family of my own, I would have accepted it, in the absence of being able to do anything else; but I haven't had one, thank Heavens. The only relative I've ever known, my brother, died in America, something like twenty years ago. A family? Children, you say? Doses of measles and whooping cough permanently cooped up in my home, to be followed later on by punishments of a hundred lines from school masters, secondary school, until the little brats eventually take it into their heads, in their turn, to have me pass for a granddad! What have I done to you to deserve such a fate?

CARBONNEL: Well, there's a homage to the virtues of pure selfishness, or my name isn't Carbonnel.

FRONTIGNAC: Eh! My God, yes! But isn't selfishness to be found everywhere? Love? It's nothing but selfishness between two people. Parenthood? Selfishness among three, or four, or fifty as in old Priam's household. Philanthropy? Unlimited selfishness. Friendship? Selfishness without reward: our poor impoverished nature has only a meagre quantity of affection to dispense; divide it up between a wife, children, a mistress, a distant cousin. Ah! What a fine share each one will have. On the other hand, what lovelier, finer position to be in than to be an orphan, and what's more, an orphaned bachelor! Nothing above, nothing below. No grandparents who are too slow, no parents too hurried. Neither past nor future! Nothing but the present!

EVELINA: He's positively charming!

ROQUAMOR: (*Aside.*) Now there's one gentleman I plan to keep a close eye on. (*The refrain of a waltz can be heard.*)

ANTONIA: Ah! Here is a waltz which summons us to dance. Gentlemen … (*They rise.*)

FRONTIGNAC: (*To Madeleine.*) I take it, then, Mademoiselle, that your decision is final?

MADELEINE: Absolutely final.

ANTONIA: Well, in any case, do come along with us, my dear child, it will amuse you at least to watch the others dancing.

ROQUAMOR: I wouldn't be too unhappy to be able to see a little of how people dance in my own home.

EVELINA: (*In a low voice, passing close to Frontignac.*) Stanislas … I must speak with you.

CARBONNEL: (*Offering his arm to Antonia.*) My beautiful lady … (*Antonia, Evelina, Madeleine, Roquamor, Carbonnel and the guests exit to the rear of the stage.*)

SCENE V

FRONTIGNAC, MARCANDIER.

FRONTIGNAC: (*Sitting down.*) Whew!

MARCANDIER: My God! What oratory gifts you possess! I've never seen you so eloquent.

FRONTIGNAC: I was speaking with conviction. (*He begins fanning himself with his handkerchief.*)

MARCANDIER: You're sweating.

FRONTIGNAC: A little hot, that's all.

MARCANDIER: (*Aside.*) Now there's an idea! If only I could ...! (*In a loud voice.*) It's smothering hot in here... suppose I was to let in a little bit of fresh air ... What do you think?

FRONTIGNAC: As you wish.

MARCANDIER: (*Opening a window and coming back to sit down beside Frontignac.*) That's better! At least we can breathe now!

FRONTIGNAC: Thank you.

MARCANDIER: (*Aside.*) I don't wish him any ill, but there now, truly! A nice little dose of tuberculosis ... (*In a loud voice.*) Well now, is that better?

FRONTIGNAC: Oh! Very much so!

MARCANDIER: (*Aside.*) Hold on, hold on! That's a rather cool breeze! (*In a loud voice.*) Frontignac, will you allow me to speak frankly to you?

FRONTIGNAC: Please do.

MARCANDIER: Well, the thing is ... you are tiring yourself out too much, you're going to make yourself ill. (*Frontignac looks at him with astonishment. Aside.*) Good grief, what's that I can feel in my back? (*In a loud voice.*) You know how much of an interest I have in you. (*He represses a sneeze.*)

FRONTIGNAC: A ten per cent rate of interest.

MARCANDIER: That's exactly what I'm talking about! Don't you think that, where I come from, matters of the heart take priority over ... (*He represses another sneeze.*)

FRONTIGNAC: But, my dear Monsieur Marcandier, we are friends; there's no need to feel uncomfortable, beat around the bush or stand on ceremony.

MARCANDIER: I do feel a little uncomfortable, as it happens ... (*He represses yet another sneeze.*)

FRONTIGNAC: Good heavens! You've been suppressing a terrible desire to sneeze for the past half-hour; it **IS** acceptable to sneeze in polite company, I can assure you ...

MARCANDIER: But, I swear to you... (*Once more, he tries to hold back, but this time he doesn't succeed and lets forth a formidable sneeze.*)

FRONTIGNAC: (*Laughing.*) God bless you!

MARCANDIER: (*Furious, standing up.*) Devil of a man! Now it's I who have got a cold! Brr ... brr ... (*Aside.*) This only happens to me, and I'm supposed to be immune to these draughts of cold air! (*He exits the stage, continuing to sneeze.*)

SCENE VI

FRONTIGNAC, *then* SAVINIEN.

FRONTIGNAC: (*Delighted.*) That good old Monsieur Marcandier! He imagines that I can't see through his little game. (*He stands up.*) But that's no reason to allow these ladies to catch cold as well … Let's close the window. (*He goes to close the window.*)

SAVINIEN: (*Outside, offstage.*) No need to announce my arrival. (*He comes on stage. In a low voice, aside.*) The hardest part is over; I've got here, so here I am in the place I'm supposed to be. Provided that Madeleine is here. The only thing I have to make sure of now, is not to run into the master of the house, who doesn't know who I am, of course.

FRONTIGNAC: (*Coming back downstage after closing the window and encountering Savinien who brushes against him.*) Hey! You clumsy oaf!

SAVINIEN: (*Greeting him.*) Sir!

FRONTIGNAC: Where has that fellow come out of?

SAVINIEN: (*Aside.*) Time to discreetly lose ourselves in this crowd. (*He exits stage left.*)

SCENE VII

FRONTIGNAC, ANTONIA.

FRONTIGNAC: (*Watching him exit.*) What a funny little fellow he is!

ANTONIA: (*Entering from the rear.*) And what do I have here; well, if it isn't Monsieur de Frontignac, still in this little drawing room … you seem to be avoiding us!

FRONTIGNAC: Well, would you believe it, Madame, something told me I'd have the pleasure of meeting you here.

ANTONIA: Is this just silly, idle talk on your part?

FRONTIGNAC: I speak from the heart.

ANTONIA: Be quiet, Sir; if anybody were to overhear you! This drawing room is not accustomed to such avowals.

FRONTIGNAC: Well! I'll speak more quietly in that case. (*He draws closer to her.*)

ANTONIA: My husband is a terrible man; the slightest suspicion, and I would be lost!

FRONTIGNAC: Unfortunately, Madame, you have nothing to feel guilty about.

ANTONIA: You think it nothing that I lent my ear to your professions of love? Moreover, and make no mistake about this, this is not Madame Roquamor who listens to you now, it is, rather, the charity organiser who has come to thank you for your generous gifts to her poverty-stricken charges.

FRONTIGNAC: For those twenty-five concert tickets and for my twenty-five gold coins, just think to yourself, Madame, it is I who am obliged to you. I can't promise you that I shall go to applaud your music, but have I not been repaid a hundredfold by that charming postscript which your divine hand was kind enough to add to the letter seeking donations?

ANTONIA: That postscript? But what did it say? I no longer remember.

FRONTIGNAC: (*In a sparkling manner.*) She has forgotten it. "Please call one of these evenings; that is the time when I entertain those who love me."

ANTONIA: Really! I wrote that. (*Aside.*) How foolhardy of me!

FRONTIGNAC: (*Very tenderly.*) Ah! Madame, am I not one of your poor charges, that I have the right to come to you, in my turn, to seek your charity?

ANTONIA: Am I to believe you? How many women before me have you spoken to in these terms?

FRONTIGNAC: And what if that was the case! What if I have, in the past, conjugated that sweet verb "to love" with others besides you? If I love you now, is it not because I find you charming and adorable above all others?

ANTONIA: Be quiet! Be quiet!

FRONTIGNAC: Ah! Please understand, Madame, when I am with you, I know not what I say or what I do … my head is all aflame, it is no longer blood which courses through my veins, but bright shining silver, and fire! (*He seizes her hand and kisses it.*)

ANTONIA: But, Sir! …

SCENE VIII

THE SAME CHARACTERS AS IN THE PREVIOUS SCENE; SAVINIEN.

SAVINIEN: (*Appearing to the rear of the stage at the very moment that Frontignac is kissing Antonia's hand.*) Oh!

ANTONIA: (*Uttering a cry.*) Ah! (*She runs off stage, to the left.*)

SCENE IX

FRONTIGNAC, SAVINIEN.

FRONTIGNAC: Gadzooks! (*Going towards Savinien, speaking very loudly.*) Sir!

SAVINIEN: (*Very politely.*) The card-games room is through here, isn't it?

FRONTIGNAC: Yes, Sir. (*Aside.*) Actually, he may not have seen anything!

SAVINIEN: (*Saluting.*) Many thanks. (*Aside.*) I still haven't caught sight of her. (*He exits.*)

SCENE X

FRONTIGNAC, *then* EVELINA.

FRONTIGNAC: (*Speaking to himself.*) What matter! That's one little gentleman who doesn't appeal to me with his polite airs. (*Seeing Evelina who appears to the rear.*) Evelina! I had forgotten about her …

EVELINA: Stanislas, you no longer love me!

FRONTIGNAC: Not so loud, Madame! If anybody were to overhear you! This drawing room is not accustomed to the declaration of such secrets!

EVELINA: Now Stanislas, this is no joking matter; our stolen moments are precious. This existence of lies and deceit is weighing heavily upon me; it's killing me! We must finish with it: last night, when Monsieur Marcandier kissed me as he lay down in bed, I could feel myself blushing … he put on his cotton nightcap with a degree of trust which touched me. What can I tell you? He asked me the cause of my distress, and I began to stammer! … One more ordeal like that and I confess, I shall be lost!

FRONTIGNAC: What?!

EVELINA: There's only one way to put an end to this torment. Let's run away together. Let us go and seek, under other skies, the happiness which is denied us here!

FRONTIGNAC: Ah! But no! Ah! But no!

EVELINA: You're hesitating?

FRONTIGNAC: Not in the least; I'm refusing!

EVELINA: Ah! Stanislas! You don't love me! You have never loved me!

FRONTIGNAC: (*Very **faux**-dramatically.*) Ah! Evelina, what have you just said? Are you not afraid of piercing this heart of mine which belongs to you alone? (*Aside.*) I was more convincing in this role of mine a little earlier. (*In a loud voice, with a sparkling manner.*) I don't love you! I don't love her!

EVELINA: Ah! Already, that sounds better …

FRONTIGNAC: Where else would I find such pretty eyes, such a charming figure, such a snow-white hand? …

EVELINA: Ah! You ungrateful treacherous wretch! Whenever you want …

FRONTIGNAC: (*Aside.*) Must I? (*He looks round.*) Nobody! Bah! It's an answer for everything and it costs so little. (*Aloud.*) Shoulders asking to be kissed. (*He leans forward over her shoulder and kisses it.*)

SCENE XI

THE SAME CHARACTERS; SAVINIEN.

SAVINIEN: (*Witnessing the kiss.*) Oh!

EVELINA: (*Uttering a cry.*) Ah! (*She runs offstage.*)

SCENE XII

SAVINIEN, FRONTIGNAC.

SAVINIEN: (*In a quietly-spoken aside.*) Not this fellow again! This makes it twice in one evening!

FRONTIGNAC: Confound it! (*Going over in a brisk, lively fashion towards Savinien.*) Sir …

SAVINIEN: (*Greeting him very politely.*) Sir …

FRONTIGNAC: Are you doing this deliberately, by any chance?

SAVINIEN: Doing ***what*** deliberately … what are you talking about?

FRONTIGNAC: This business of greeting me so insistently and repeatedly … I have no idea who you are.

SAVINIEN: Nor do I have any idea who ***you*** are! …

FRONTIGNAC: Ah! (*Aside.*) I don't like this young whippersnapper one little bit, he doesn't at all appeal to me. (*He exists to the rear of the stage.*)

SCENE XIII

SAVINIEN, followed by ROQUAMOR.

SAVINIEN: (*Alone.*) Now there's a gentleman who certainly puts his evenings to good use … I can understand the workings of polite society under these conditions … Whereas, for me … Ah! The position of a young man who arrives at a ball without having been invited to it, has something intrinsically and deeply upsetting about it … I feel as if everybody is looking at me and wondering what right I have to be here; as for me, I'm avoiding everyone, especially the master of the house; but never mind! We others, we Americans, we have no doubts or uncertainties about anything, and if only I could catch sight of Madeleine … And yet she ***did*** tell me that she would come, and that is why … (*He* *catches sight of Roquamor, who appears to the rear.*) Ah! There's somebody!

ROQUAMOR: (*Speaking to one of the servants.*) Go easy on the refreshments, in the name of God!

SAVINIEN: (*Aside.*) Oh! It's the master of the house. (*He turns round to make himself inconspicuous, and starts humming with his back turned.*)

ROQUAMOR: Ah! One of my guests! By Jove, at least I'm going to get to know who I'm entertaining. (*He greets Savinien, who continues to stand with his back turned to him.*) Sir!

SAVINIEN: What studied elegance in the very smallest of things! What refinement of taste! What a charming ball! How happy one feels in this place, at the home of a man of wit!

ROQUAMOR: (*Aside.*) Ah! Well, there's ***one*** person at least who happens to be polite. (*In a loud voice.*) Sir!

SAVINIEN: (*Looking at the walls.*) Ah! Those delightful pictures!

ROQUAMOR: (*Aside.*) He does have taste, that's quite evident, but why does he have his back turned to me? (*Loudly.*) Sir. I say … Sir!

SAVINIEN: This painting is positively lifelike! One would almost imagine that it's about to … pull a face.

ROQUAMOR: What?!

SAVINIEN: It's a monkey!

ROQUAMOR: (*Furiously.*) My portrait!

SAVINIEN: Oops … oh dear! (*He slips away, exiting stage right.*)

ROQUAMOR: A monkey, indeed! (*Walking back toward the rear.*) Ah! If this happens to me just once more … (*Exiting.*) I'll give him a monkey, indeed!

SCENE XIV

SAVINIEN, followed by MADELEINE.

SAVINIEN: (*Coming back into the living room through a different door.*) You have to be on the lookout around here and avoid danger, God damn it! You have to be on your guard. But I'm now in a fine pickle: he's going to have me thrown out! (*Madeleine appears to the rear.*) Ah! Mademoiselle Madeleine!

MADELEINE: (*Coming down towards him.*) Monsieur Savinien!

SAVINIEN: At last!

MADELEINE: So, you managed to have yourself formally announced and introduced?

SAVINIEN: I announced myself, and in a rather novel way, I can assure you!

MADELEINE: But …

SAVINIEN: We other sons of noble America, we shall suffer no uncertainty, we are as free as our mother country. (*He tries to hug her.*)

MADELEINE: (*Extricating herself from his grasp.*) So I see.

SAVINIEN: My word, I must say that I was becoming furiously bored, and really missing you, waiting to see you at this ball.

MADELEINE: And how do you think I felt! (*She stops speaking.*)

SAVINIEN: Oh! There's no need to stop speaking! And yet, you can't have been short of dance partners inviting you onto the floor?

MADELEINE: I didn't dance.

SAVINIEN: Dear Madeleine! (*He embraces her tightly.*) So, will you grant me the first waltz?

MADELEINE: Of course.

SAVINIEN: The first polka?

MADELEINE: Yes.

SAVINIEN: The first quadrille?

MADELEINE: (*Showing him her dance card.*) I've arranged my dance schedule in such a way that the entire evening has been reserved for you and you alone. (*She inadvertently drops her dance card on the sofa.*)

SAVINIEN: What a good person you are! How I love you!

MADELEINE: Really and truly?

SAVINIEN: Ever since I set foot on European soil, ever since I first laid eyes on you!

MADELEINE: Well then, my uncle is here; we'll have to speak with him.

SAVINIEN: Dear, oh dear, oh dear! The fact of the matter is that I have no fortune, no elevated social position to offer you or him …

MADELEINE: I have no need of any such thing.

SAVINIEN: How kind she is! But as for your uncle, he'll certainly have need of it … If only you knew what hard fellows they are, these uncles!

MADELEINE: How do you happen to be acquainted with such a fact, since you are without any family?

SAVINIEN: Hold on … that's it, you see! You've reminded me of something … but yes! I too ***do*** have an uncle, I must in fact possess an uncle, unless he is dead … but where? An uncle whom I've never seen and who is unaware of my very existence, for he doesn't even know that his brother was married.

MADELEINE: I will hardly be able to help you find him, since I am as much a newcomer and stranger in Paris as you are. My poor Monsieur Savinien!

SAVINIEN: Poor! Come on, now! I am armed with courage and a strong work ethic, and am loved by the most ravishing young woman … Poor! My dear Madeleine … (*The prelude to a waltz is heard; he catches her round the waist.*) When I hold you to my heart, when … upon my word, this is too bad but I cannot help myself! (*He kisses her.*)

MADELEINE: Ah! (*Just as Savinien is kissing Madeleine and leading her to the dance floor, Frontignac appears to the right.*)

SCENE XV

FRONTIGNAC, followed by CARBONNEL, MARCANDIER, ROQUAMOR.

FRONTIGNAC: (*Alone.*) Him again! So this boudoir is turning out to be a right little love nest, indeed! Ah, the rogue! And that little lady refusing to dance with Frontignac! Ah! This won't do at all! This little fellow needs to be taught a lesson … In the meantime … (*He sits down and sees Madeleine's dance card.*) Hold on! What's that? A young lady's dance card? But who can it belong to? Let's have a look. (*He opens the card and rises in a brusque, lively manner.*) Ah! Well! Ah! Good! Ah! Well done! Ah! Magnificent! Ah! Splendid!

MARCANDIER: (*Returning on stage accompanied by Roquamor and Carbonnel.*) Charming! Charming!

ROQUAMOR: Ah! If this happens to me just once more!

FRONTIGNAC: Hey, Carbonnel! Come over here a minute, will you?

CARBONNEL: What is it?

FRONTIGNAC: (*Showing him the dance card.*) Does this look familiar to you?

CARBONNEL: My niece's dance card.

FRONTIGNAC: So it belongs to Mademoiselle Madeleine; I've made a lucky discovery. In any case, take a look at the dancer's name.

CARBONNEL: What do you mean?

FRONTIGNAC: Read it! Read it!

CARBONNEL: (*Reading aloud.*) First quadrille, Monsieur Savinien.

FRONTIGNAC: Go on.

CARBONNEL: First polka, M. Savinien! – What is this about?

FRONTIGNAC: Keep going!

CARBONNEL: First waltz, M. Savinien! Ah! Bah!

FRONTIGNAC: Second quadrille, M. Savinien. Second polka, M. Savinien. Second waltz, M. Savinien. Always M. Savinien. Thirty-five times: M. Savinien.

MARCANDIER: A lot of Savinien.

ROQUAMOR: Too much Savinien!

CARBONNEL: What does all this mean?

FRONTIGNAC: Well might he ask! There is one little diary which speaks louder than many volumes. I daresay the name in it has a body, a face and perhaps even a moustache.

MARCANDIER: Thirty-five Saviniens!

CARBONNEL: Ah! I'm going to find out what exactly is going on here!

SCENE XVI

THE SAME CHARACTERS; SAVINIEN. (*He seems extremely busy and is searching amongst all the furniture.*)

FRONTIGNAC: Him again! By Jove, it couldn't be anybody but he!

SAVINIEN: (*Aside.*) She must have left it somewhere around here.

FRONTIGNAC: (*Aside.*) Search, my dear fellow, search!

ROQUAMOR: Well, if it isn't the monkey!

MARCANDIER: What? What monkey?

SAVINIEN: (*Catching sight of the dance card being held by Frontignac, aside.*) Ah! (*Loud.*) I beg your pardon, Sir, but you're holding an object there that …

FRONTIGNAC: That you're looking for?

SAVINIEN: That I'm looking for.

FRONTIGNAC: I say, Carbonnel, please be good enough to ask this gentleman whether, by any chance, his name might not happen to be Savinien …

CARBONNEL: Indeed.

SAVINIEN: (*To Frontignac.*) I can see, Sir, that you have been indiscreet enough as to …

CARBONNEL: But Savinien is a baptismal name, and Monsieur Roquamor will be kind enough to inform us …

ROQUAMOR: (*In a loud, excited voice.*) Me! You mean I may actually be acquainted with somebody in my own home?

FRONTIGNAC: Oh, I see what's going on here. You do sometimes run into these lowly young men who manage to worm their way into polite society, coming from God only knows where, living from God knows what … but desirous, above all else, of remaining anonymous …

SAVINIEN: Sir!

MARCANDIER: (*Aside.*) Good! Things are starting to get heated around here!

ROQUAMOR: (*To Savinien.*) Your name, Sir?

SAVINIEN: As you wish. It is your right to know who I am, and you shall read my name on the card which I am now about to hand to this gentleman. (*He points to Frontignac.*)

MARCANDIER: (*Aside.*) A duel!

SAVINIEN: (*To Frontignac.*) As for you, Sir, I shall teach you that a young lady's secrets are a sacred thing, and after what I've seen of you, I would have expected more discretion on your part in connection with what you have seen of ***me***.

FRONTIGNAC: Sir!

ROQUAMOR: What has he seen?

MARCANDIER: What has he seen?

CARBONNEL: Stay calm! Stay calm!

MARCANDIER: (*Aside.*) Keep going! Keep going!

FRONTIGNAC: I want to teach this young fellow a lesson …

SAVINIEN: And I want to teach one to this old fellow …

FRONTIGNAC: You have gone too far, Sir … Here is my card.

SAVINIEN: And here is mine … (*They exchange cards.*)

ROQUAMOR: Really, gentlemen, in my home, such scandalous, outrageous conduct!

FRONTIGNAC: (*Crumples Savinien's card, then looks at it, becomes astonished and returns it to him.*) There is some mistake here, Sir!

SAVINIEN: (*Behaving likewise with Frontignac's card.*) It's correct. (*They exchange the cards once again.*)

FRONTIGNAC: (*Creasing the card and looking at it in the same way as before.*) Again!

SAVINIEN: (*Behaving likewise with Frontignac's card.*) What! (*A third exchange of cards takes place.*)

FRONTIGNAC: (*Reading.*) S. de Frontignac!

SAVINIEN: (*Reading.*) S. de Frontignac!

FRONTIGNAC: Confound and dash it, man! I do not acknowledge any other Frontignac but myself!

SAVINIEN: And me too, if you please: Savinien de Frontignac, son of Joseph de Frontignac.

FRONTIGNAC: (*Stunned.*) Who died twenty years ago, in New York!

SAVINIEN: One and the same.

FRONTIGNAC: (*Suddenly sagging downwards into a seat.*) A nephew!

SAVINIEN: My uncle!

ROQUAMOR, MARCANDIER, CARBONNEL: His nephew!

SCENE XVII

THE SAME, ANTONIA, EVELINA, MADELEINE, GUESTS. (*Running up to investigate all this commotion.*)

ANTONIA: What on earth is going on?

ROQUAMOR: It's this gentleman here who has just become an uncle.

FRONTIGNAC: A nephew in my life!

MARCANDIER: (*To Evelina.*) Let's take our leave; let's leave these two to the joys of their family reunion.

CARBONNEL: (*To Madeleine, giving her his arm.*) Come along, young lady, we shall have matters to discuss. (*The assembled group begins to leave.*)

FRONTIGNAC: (*Still overcome with astonishment.*) An uncle! I am an uncle!

FIRST GUEST: (*To Roquamor, giving him a coin and a number.*) Here you are, my good man, there's twenty sous, go and get my jacket.

ROQUAMOR: (*Exasperated.*) Oh!

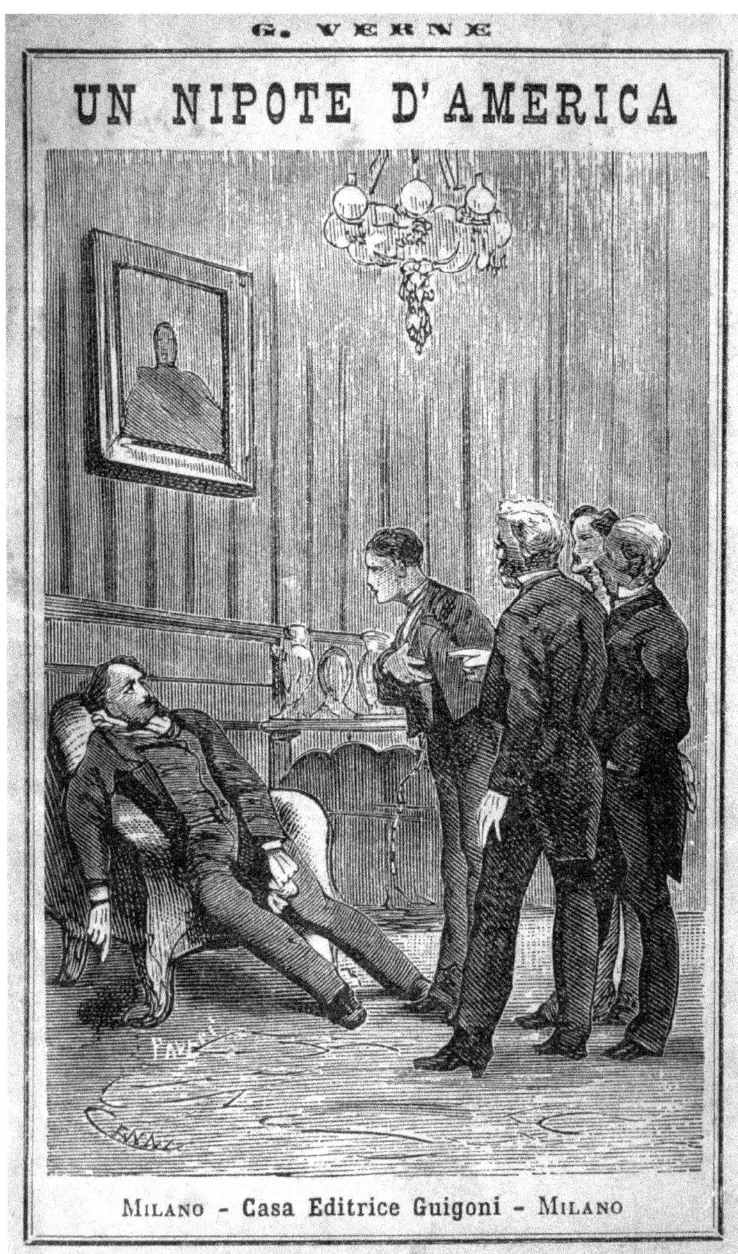

Cover of a 19th century Italian translation.

ACT TWO

A small living room at Frontignac's home. Doors to the side, a door to the rear.

SCENE I

FRONTIGNAC, then DOMINIQUE.

FRONTIGNAC: (*Wearing a morning coat, enters from the right and calling out.*) Dominique!

DOMINIQUE: (*From offstage.*) Sir!

FRONTIGNAC: (*Calling.*) Dominique!

DOMINIQUE: (*Offstage.*) Sir!

FRONTIGNAC: By Jove! … I can hear you perfectly well replying "Sir!" But that isn't sufficient. (*Shouting.*) Dominique! …

DOMINIQUE: (*Appearing at the door to the left.*) Sir has not summoned me, by any chance?

FRONTIGNAC: For the past hour!

DOMINIQUE: I'd heard you well enough … Sir has slept badly?

FRONTIGNAC: I have … I have … Look, it's none of your concern. I am expecting company to lunch.

DOMINIQUE: A lady?

FRONTIGNAC: No!

DOMINIQUE: A man?

FRONTIGNAC: No!

DOMINIQUE: (*Astonished.*) What? (*A little stung in his pride.*) Ah! Sir is harbouring secrets, it seems.

FRONTIGNAC: It is neither a woman, nor a man … it's … a nephew!

DOMINIQUE: Sir is having a little joke?

FRONTIGNAC: You think I'm joking?!

DOMINIQUE: I'm well aware that Sir is as much an orphan as Adam himself, and unable to have given himself a nephew … now, as for a godson, I'm not saying that …

FRONTIGNAC: You have a high opinion of me, you do!

DOMINIQUE: Sir is being serious! Ah! But no! Well … this wasn't part of our agreement.

FRONTIGNAC: What exactly are you saying, Monsieur Dominique?

DOMINIQUE: Dash it! A master who is a bachelor, that isn't the most advantageous situation to be in! But if Sir is today taking it into his head to fantasize that he's an uncle … Ah! But no! Ah! But no, really!

FRONTIGNAC: And you think this whole matter is amusing for me? A big strapping nephew who lands on my doorstep from America without a word of warning … Well, at the end of the day, the least I can do is invite him to lunch, and … I'm expecting him to arrive at any moment.

DOMINIQUE: Ah! So it's like that, is it … Well! Sir could easily have consulted me …

FRONTIGNAC: That shall be for some other occasion.

DOMINIQUE: What should I serve you, Sir?

FRONTIGNAC: Oh! … a very simple lunch … Nothing at all if you like … You understand, I'm obliged to show hospitality under my roof to my nephew, so I'm entertaining him, and that's all …

DOMINIQUE: Very well … and what about wine? …

FRONTIGNAC: The little Beaujolais that's just been bottled will do nicely.

DOMINIQUE: Gosh! … it's young.

FRONTIGNAC: My nephew, too, is young. (*The sound of the doorbell ringing is heard.*) That'll be him; please show him in.

DOMINIQUE: Yes, Sir. (*Aside.*) A nephew – now that's ***all*** we needed. (*He exits the stage.*)

SCENE II

FRONTIGNAC, then DOMINIQUE and SAVINIEN.

FRONTIGNAC: (*Alone.*) One has obligations towards members of one's family, I accept that! Let us do things properly, but without any enthusiasm.

DOMINIQUE: (*Announcing the visitor.*) Monsieur Savinien de Frontignac.

FRONTIGNAC: Lunch!

DOMINIQUE: Yes, Sir. (*Aside.*) As if he couldn't have just stayed where he was in America, that fellow. (*He goes out.*)

SAVINIEN: (*Very pleasantly and politely.*) Good afternoon, Uncle. (*He offers his hand.*)

FRONTIGNAC: (*A little coldly.*) Good afternoon, nephew. (*Aside.*) Uncle! Uncle! I don't like that title … It makes me feel old …

SAVINIEN: I hope I'm not disturbing you?

FRONTIGNAC: No!

SAVINIEN: You must agree, Uncle, that our meeting occurred in a really unusual way! My word, aren't I the awkward fellow to go and throw myself into two charming little *tête-à-tête*, I do declare! You must have been wishing hellfire and brimstone upon me, eh?

FRONTIGNAC: The thing is …

SAVINIEN: Oh! No need to feel embarrassed, and you were right …

FRONTIGNAC: I admit that, at first, this bombshell did produce a rather strange effect on me … that of a cold shower, but now …

SAVINIEN: Now?

FRONTIGNAC: I've recovered. It even appears that this thing of discovering a nephew you never even knew existed, gives you one hell of an appetite, as I'm now absolutely ravenous!

SAVINIEN: I say! Me too! So there is fellow feeling between us …

FRONTIGNAC: (*calling*): Dominique!

DOMINIQUE: (*Bringing in a table with food and drink.*) Lunch is served, Sir.

FRONTIGNAC: Well, let's eat, nephew!

SAVINIEN: Let's eat!

FRONTIGNAC: (*Aside.*) I do declare, he seems to be quite the *bon viveur* who appreciates the finer things in life, and since I've had to inherit a long-lost nephew, it might as well be this fellow as any other.

SAVINIEN: (*Aside.*) Quite an eccentric fellow, this uncle of mine … but a good man at the back of it all.

FRONTIGNAC: So, what on earth was that brother of mine thinking of when he didn't let me know he'd got married or that a son had been born to him?

SAVINIEN: My goodness! Uncle, I could hardly have let you know myself …

FRONTIGNAC: That is true.

SAVINIEN: Good health, Uncle … (*He drinks and makes a slight grimace.*)

FRONTIGNAC: It seems that my Beaujolais is not very mature. (*Calling in a low voice.*) Hum! Hum! Dominique!

DOMINIQUE: Sir!

FRONTIGNAC: (*In a low voice.*) Couldn't you give us something a little nicer … some Beaune, for instance?

DOMINIQUE: Pooh! Sir, for a nephew!

FRONTIGNAC: Yes, but there's one thing I hadn't thought of: I have to drink it too!

DOMINIQUE: That's right: Beaune it is, then.

SAVINIEN: (*Having overheard this exchange.*) No, no, … don't change anything on my account, this little wine will do. I don't wish to disturb your routine in any way.

FRONTIGNAC: Huh! …

SAVINIEN: Ah! Uncle, it is only on that condition that I agree to make peace with you.

FRONTIGNAC: What? What?!

SAVINIEN: I ask nothing of you, I want nothing, you've been living your own life, I don't wish to cause any upheaval in it … I shall be your companion, if you will allow me, but a source of awkwardness, never! …

FRONTIGNAC: (*Aside.*) Hold on a moment! Hold on! Hold on! A companion! I prefer the sound of that, it makes me feel younger. (*Dominique returns and places another bottle on the table. In a loud voice.*) To my nephew's good health. (*He pours wine for his nephew.*)

SAVINIEN: To your health … Mmm. This wine tastes nicer.

FRONTIGNAC: Yes, I do believe so! I agree that one doesn't get to my age—even though I haven't got one foot in the grave just yet—without acquiring certain habits which would be rather unpleasant to have to suddenly dispense with … At the same time, when one is faced with new obligations …

SAVINIEN: Obligations? What sort of obligations are you referring to, Uncle? It is not I, I imagine, who is putting them on you. If you say one more word on that subject, Uncle, I shall say my goodbyes, take my leave of you with a bow and you shall never see me again, it will be our ***Adieu!***

FRONTIGNAC: Ah! There now, but he's … you're quite the charmer! My word, yes indeed … can we be on first-name terms? Is that alright with you?

SAVINIEN : (*Shaking his hand.*) That would give me great pleasure!

FRONTIGNAC: Hell, me too! But what was it that I'd been saying to myself earlier? The thing is, I'm now delighted … Word of honor … I missed him … I missed you!

SAVINIEN: Uncle! …

FRONTIGNAC: He couldn't be any more perfect than if I'd ordered him custom-built! Hum! Hum! Dominique? …

DOMINIQUE: Sir!

FRONTIGNAC: Dominique is going to bring us a bottle of our finest Chambertin.

DOMINIQUE: What …!

FRONTIGNAC: Two bottles! And if you answer me back …

DOMINIQUE: Alright, alright, whatever! (*Aside.*) What on earth has gotten into him? (*He goes out.*)

SAVINIEN: It seems to me, my dear Uncle, that you are cheerfully descending the river of life …

FRONTIGNAC: The current is so hard to ascend in the opposite direction! And moreover, woman is such a charming creature, though steeped in vice and faults … Ah! On that subject … do people fall in love in America?

SAVINIEN: But of course!

FRONTIGNAC: Let's examine the matter more closely. Have you noticed, Savinien, that women borrow three quarters of their charming qualities from the environment in which they are placed? At twenty years old, they wish to be loved in the full light of day; at thirty, they prefer to be loved under softer lighting and, at forty, it's after nightfall. A blonde insists that she be adored in an oratory all hung with blue damask; a brunette in a sanctuary padded with yellow damask … Furthermore, beyond this door, to the right and to the left, are the sought-after temples.

SAVINIEN: Oh! Oh! …

FRONTIGNAC: Laugh if you will, but if somebody were to offer me twenty thousand francs to leave this apartment, I'd refuse!

DOMINIQUE: (*Entering.*) The Chambertin you requested, Sir.

SAVINIEN: It's very nice wine, my uncle's Chambertin …

FRONTIGNAC: Yes, I like to think so … and now, a cigar …

SAVINIEN: No! Hold on a minute! Get a load of the taste of these!

FRONTIGNAC: They're excellent!

SAVINIEN: Well, my dear Uncle, I've brought two boxes of them especially for you.

FRONTIGNAC: You joker! You didn't know me … but here's me babbling on for the past hour, when I ought to be talking about you and finding out more about you … and your plans for the future. Let me see, then; so, what exactly is it that you do?

SAVINIEN: Whatever it takes to earn eighteen hundred francs a year.

FRONTIGNAC: You must really have your nose to the grindstone. I'd like to be able to do something for you …

SAVINIEN: Good heavens! We'd agreed not to bring up that subject … I didn't seek you out, I didn't happen upon you just to …

FRONTIGNAC: Let it not be said that …

SAVINIEN: I say, Uncle, even though I refuse your offer of money, there is still one big favour you **can** do for me …

FRONTIGNAC: Name it … loud and clear!

SAVINIEN: There is a certain young lady! …

FRONTIGNAC: Whom you love … and who loves you … perfect … we'll get our hands on her!

SAVINIEN: The thing is …

FRONTIGNAC: We'll snatch her away … A blue or yellow boudoir?

SAVINIEN: Before it gets that far, I'd prefer to try another method … I should like to marry her.

FRONTIGNAC: (*Scandalised.*) Marry her? You! … An American, a young man, a lusty fellow! … Yet your intentions do seem honorable.

SAVINIEN: In America, there are no other types of intentions.

FRONTIGNAC: Enroll in my school and I'll help you cultivate other types!

SAVINIEN: No, Uncle, never … moreover, I am madly in love.

FRONTIGNAC: All the more reason to go a bit mad, live a little, be extravagant …

SAVINIEN: Extravagant? Oh! Whatever you wish … but … but … as you say … with honorable intentions.

FRONTIGNAC: At least you're a novel customer, I'll give you that. However, I'm saying nothing. Tell me what favour you want me to do for you.

SAVINIEN: You are acquainted with Madeleine's uncle … Monsieur Charbonnel?

FRONTIGNAC: Too right I'm acquainted with him! Another old rascal just like me … Indeed, he lives right here in this very building, on the floor above … Savinien …

SAVINIEN: Uncle!

FRONTIGNAC: The matter is decided, then. Going … going … gone! No regrets?

SAVINIEN: None whatsoever!

FRONTIGNAC: That's settled, then! (*To Dominique.*) Dominique, will you ask M. Carbonnel to please be good enough to come down here to see me at once? (*Dominique goes out to carry out this order.*)

SAVINIEN: What do you intend to do?

FRONTIGNAC: Why, to make your proposal on your behalf, of course! Surely you aren't backing out now? Are you going back to having nobler sentiments? No! Well then, trust me, I know what I'm doing!

SAVINIEN: If you were to jeopardize …

FRONTIGNAC: A – ahem – **business** affair? Never! Though I can't speak for women …

SCENE III

FRONTIGNAC, SAVINIEN, CARBONNEL.

CARBONNEL: You asked to see me? Eh! But, if it isn't your nephew from America; a charming young fellow.

SAVINIEN: Sir!

FRONTIGNAC: Do you think so?

CARBONNEL: Most assuredly!

FRONTIGNAC: Choose your response carefully and weigh your words judiciously! You have just said of my nephew Savinien that he is a charming young fellow. And I don't wish to have to take you for a traitor to his word. Take a look. (*To Savinien.*) Turn round! There! Walk a few steps.

SAVINIEN: But …

FRONTIGNAC: What's the matter; have you forgotten how to walk? Take a few steps; there! Now turn around …

CARBONNEL: But what … ?

FRONTIGNAC: Do you still maintain your favorable opinion?

CARBONNEL: What opinion?

FRONTIGNAC: That he's charming!

CARBONNEL: Well, yes…

FRONTIGNAC: You can see how he's built … a true Frontignac, all the way from America … A wide chest, a good stomach, fit as a fiddle, all thirty-two teeth his own, and no more than that.

CARBONNEL: Is he for sale or something?

FRONTIGNAC: Precisely! (*To Savinien.*) You may be seated. (*To Carbonnel.*) I have the great honor of asking you, on behalf of my nephew Savinien de Frontignac, for the hand in marriage of Mademoiselle Madeleine, your niece.

CARBONNEL: Ah … bah!

SAVINIEN: Uncle!

FRONTIGNAC: Well?

CARBONNEL: But …

FRONTIGNAC: You give your consent, then? Perfect! I expected nothing less from our old friendship. Savinien, you may now embrace your new uncle.

SAVINIEN: Could this be really true?

CARBONNEL: Please, young man, allow me to …

FRONTIGNAC: What?

CARBONNEL: What the devil!

FRONTIGNAC: And …. ?

CARBONNEL: Give me time to get my breath back!

FRONTIGNAC: Breathe then, Sir. So, has our deal been concluded?

CARBONNEL: You certainly have a way with words when it comes to asking people for the hand in marriage of their niece!

FRONTIGNAC: And it's the right way; but at least nobody can say that I used violence with you … Speak, but speak quickly!

CARBONNEL: First of all, where did Monsieur Savinien meet Madeleine?

FRONTIGNAC: In Le Havre … Next?

CARBONNEL: Next … next … It's true that he is a charming fellow, I repeat that…

FRONTIGNAC: So we're agreed …

CARBONNEL: Well! Yes, on that score, I am not going back on my word. I like him, and he **is** your nephew! …

FRONTIGNAC: Savinien, embrace …

SAVINIEN: Ah! Sir …

FRONTIGNAC: (*To Savinien.*) Now, go upstairs to Carbonnel's apartment, ask for Mademoiselle Madeleine, tell her that she possesses the best of uncles, an extraordinary uncle, and bring her back down here; the least I can do is embrace my niece … Heavens, it's well due to me. (*Savinien exits hastily to the rear.*)

CARBONNEL: What is he saying? What is he saying? But no! But no! You have quite a way of doing business, don't you?

FRONTIGNAC: Of course I do! … These youngsters, they are impatient to seize happiness.

CARBONNEL: Well, if this is what makes them happy… The only matter remaining for us to attend to now is to settle the question of interest.

FRONTIGNAC: Oh! Is that really necessary? They are in love with each other, and they seek nothing more.

CARBONNEL: So it's up to us to be sensible on their behalf! My niece does not have a large fortune, merely a small farm in Normandy. And your nephew?

FRONTIGNAC: Savinien … has nothing.

CARBONNEL: What?!

FRONTIGNAC: I said, he has nothing, of course! But why are we getting into a tizzy about such trifling matters? Have you never been in love, then, Carbonnel?

CARBONNEL: This isn't about me, but about Madeleine's welfare, and this is something which makes a distinct difference to the whole situation.

FRONTIGNAC: Well! But, after all, am I not here too?

CARBONNEL: As you've been repeatedly reminding us … What are you giving to your nephew?

FRONTIGNAC: Ah! Great Scott, but now that I come to think of it … I possess nothing, personally … I have invested everything I own in a life annuity …

CARBONNEL: Are you serious?

FRONTIGNAC: A nice little idea of mine it was too … my poor Savinien! … What a selfish old git I am! Good God! I wasn't expecting this!

CARBONNEL: Oh! Oh! But then …

FRONTIGNAC: But allow me to reassure you … Though I no longer hold any property-type assets, I **do** have an income, and I have every intention of sharing my private income with Savinien.

CARBONNEL: That's all very well, for as long as you're in the land of the living … but after you pass on …

FRONTIGNAC: Let me reassure you … I don't entertain the slightest desire to …

SCENE IV

THE SAME; SAVINIEN, bringing along MADELEINE.

SAVINIEN: My dear Madeleine, let us thank this excellent uncle.

CARBONNEL: There's no point … it's all off!

FRONTIGNAC: What?!

MADELINE: Uncle!

CARBONNEL: I'm withdrawing my consent.

SAVINIEN: Sir! Ah! My poor Madeleine. (*He kisses her.*)

CARBONNEL: Do you mind ***not*** kissing my niece? Have you ever seen the likes of …

FRONTIGNAC: Carbonnel? What, these tears do not move you?

MADELEINE: I shall be forever inconsolable!

SAVINIEN: And ***I*** shall die of a broken heart! (*He kisses Madeleine.*)

CARBONNEL: (*Separating them.*) He has no respect for anything, this young American whippersnapper! Great Scott! This is altogether too much! Shake off this mortal coil and die of a broken heart, my dear Sir, if that may be some source of pleasantness to you, but you shall **not** have my niece! (*Carbonnel and Madeleine exit.*)

SCENE V

FRONTIGNAC, SAVINIEN.

FRONTIGNAC: You'll pay for this, you damned old scoundrel—I'll have my pound of flesh from you yet, Sir!

SAVINIEN: But, Uncle, can you explain to me what has brought about such a sudden change of mind on his part? Just a quarter of an hour ago, Monsieur Carbonnel had given his consent to this marriage, and now he's refusing to allow me entertain any hope whatsoever?

FRONTIGNAC: The man is an animal!

SAVINIEN: Who can have brought about such a sudden change of mind on his part?

FRONTIGNAC: Who? … Upon my word … I have no idea what it's all about!

SAVINIEN: Are you being completely truthful with me, Uncle?

FRONTIGNAC: I give you my word … Well! No! I **do** have some slight idea as to what this is all about …

SAVINIEN: Which is …?

FRONTIGNAC: Listen, Savinien, and please don't be angry with me when you hear what I have to say. First of all, I couldn't ever have had the slightest inkling that a nephew whose existence I had known nothing of, was going so suddenly arrive on my doorstep one day … a nephew who is appealing to me, whom I love … Today, I swear to you that I am truly, deeply sorry … and that, if I could only turn back the clock and have my time over again … but what do you expect? It's too late …

SAVINIEN: But still, Uncle …

FRONTIGNAC: Well! Savinien, I am nothing but a big selfish cad!

SAVINIEN: We're agreed on that …

FRONTIGNAC: Savinien, don't hold this against me, will you?

SAVINIEN: But no, no, never! A thousand times, no!

FRONTIGNAC: Well! I have invested my entire fortune in a life annuity policy. Don't you see, if I could only have guessed …

SAVINIEN: (*Interrupting him.*) But, my dear Uncle … why are you apologising? Are you not the master of your own destiny? …

FRONTIGNAC: I know, I know that only too well; but that doesn't make it any less of a misfortune and hardship – just at this very moment in our lives when some small financial sacrifice on my part might have guaranteed your happiness – to know that I can do nothing, absolutely **nothing** for you … I have thirty thousand pounds in private income, and yet they shall go to the grave with me!

SAVINIEN: An excellent idea … that money will keep you warm in the tomb …

FRONTIGNAC: What … you mean … you don't resent me?

SAVINIEN: Me! Come on, now! All I ask of you is your affection, and nothing more.

FRONTIGNAC: Why can't Carbonnel be similarly content with just that?

SAVINIEN: I understand what you mean!

FRONTIGNAC: It doesn't matter in the slightest, my dear boy … What you have just told me now, don't you see … I shall never forget it … First of all, we will begin by sharing out what we have, and then, I'll certainly have to find some means of having you marry Madeleine …

SAVINIEN: You still entertain some hope that that may still come to pass, then?

FRONTIGNAC: Do I still bear some hope? Yes, I should think so, I believe so, indeed! That young girl is perfectly charming! Hold on, listen, just leave this to me; I'm off to consult with my solicitor, and I fully intend to be able to give you some good news within the next two hours … So it's true, then, you don't begrudge me my annuity situation?

SAVINIEN: You are the best uncle anybody could possibly hope for! See you later, Uncle.

FRONTIGNAC: See you in two hours … and in the meantime, let's keep our fingers crossed! (*Savinien exits.*)

SCENE VI

FRONTIGNAC, then DOMINIQUE.

FRONTIGNAC: (*Alone.*) The devil take me if I know, as yet, how on earth I'm going to succeed with this … Ah! If anybody had told me yesterday that I, that selfish old bounder who has never once thought of anybody but himself, would suddenly be breaking with the habits of a whole lifetime, that I'd be racking my brains for the sake of some young fellow I hardly even know … Ah! If I'd been told **that** yesterday, it would have seriously, furiously astonished me … Family! It's a laughing matter, yes, a pack of idiots … This is crazy, if you like, but … I **love** him, that young fellow! And we shall see! Dominique! Dominique!

DOMINIQUE: (*Coming on stage.*) You called, Sir?

FRONTIGNAC: I am dressing to go out.

DOMINIQUE: Already! It's barely noon …

FRONTIGNAC: Have you got a problem with that?

DOMINIQUE: Dash it! Sir, I entered into service in the home of a bachelor, and now I find myself in the home of a father … It's hardly very pleasant …

FRONTIGNAC: Very well! …. Next time, I'll seek your opinion, Monsieur Dominique. But for now, bring me my hat, please …

DOMINIQUE: (*Bringing a grey hat.*) There you are, Sir!

FRONTIGNAC: A grey hat, even though it's raining! You must be joking … Give me a black hat …

DOMINIQUE: Sir is quite well aware that he no longer owns a black hat. Sir had worn the previous one for almost a month, and I sold it …

FRONTIGNAC: Alright, alright! It's okay!

DOMINIQUE: Just like clothes, gloves and ties … Ordinarily, masters bequeath something to their valets in their will … You, Sir, have put all of your fortune into a life annuity…

FRONTIGNAC: Odious, yet logical! (*To Dominique.*) We shall talk about this another time, Master Dominique; another time, we'll talk. (*He exits.*)

SCENE VII

DOMINIQUE, then MARCANDIER.

DOMINIQUE: (*Alone.*) None of these selfish old bachelors ever think of anybody else but themselves! This nephew from America was **all** we needed! It's a fine country, so why didn't he just stay over there where he was? …

MARCANDIER: (*Entering.*) Is Monsieur Frontignac at home?

DOMINIQUE: Ah! The good Monsieur Marcandier; not bad, and yourself?

MARCANDIER: Very well, thank you. And your master?

DOMINIQUE: He is washing and dressing as we speak.

MARCANDIER: I don't want to disturb him; I have time to wait. (*Aside.*) And it would be quite to my advantage, in fact, to acquire a little information while I'm waiting … (*Aloud.*) So how is he keeping, this dear old Frontignac?

DOMINIQUE: Not bad, and you?

MARCANDIER: Ah! That's good, that's good! So, he isn't a little … under the weather, perhaps …?

DOMINIQUE: But not at all!

MARCANDIER: That's great! That's great! But he ought to look after his health; we are all only mortal beings, after all.

DOMINIQUE: Him? Get his health checked out? The very sight of a doctor would be enough to make him ill!

MARCANDIER: Who said anything about a doctor? What he needs is to take care of his health without even being conscious of it, by following a healthy and invigorating diet and exercise regime. Tell me, does he wear flannel-type material at all?

DOMINIQUE: Really!

MARCANDIER: Very well! Flannel was invented by the Faculty of Medicine to swell the numbers of its ill visitors. It irritates the skin and causes rheumatism.

DOMINIQUE: Ah!

MARCANDIER: When he returns home of an evening, feeling cold, he must surely take some sort of tonic?

DOMINIQUE: No!

MARCANDIER: But how careless of him! In such cases, there's nothing like a little glass of absinthe to restore heat to the body and get the blood circulating.

DOMINIQUE: Ah! Really?

MARCANDIER: Anybody would tell you the same thing, except, of course, doctors; that wouldn't be to their advantage!

DOMINIQUE: Good to know. (*Aside.*) I must start trying that remedy out on myself. (*Aloud.*) Let's see, now. Let's not forget anything. We've said one mustn't wear flannel…

MARCANDIER: Never wear flannel!

DOMINIQUE: And a small glass of absinthe every evening…

MARCANDIER: Not too small, mind! You can even add a little every morning!

DOMINIQUE: Perfect! Two absinthes it shall be, then!

MARCANDIER: The thing is, if anything bad were ever to befall that dear old Frontignac, I would be forever inconsolable!

DOMINIQUE: Ah! My master is indeed fortunate to have such a sincere, devoted friend!

MARCANDIER: Not to mention such an enlightened and intelligent manservant!

DOMINIQUE: Ah! Here comes my master now.

MARCANDIER: Not a word about what we've just been discussing, mind.

DOMINIQUE: I should think not! (*He exits.*)

SCENE VIII

MARCANDIER, FRONTIGNAC.

FRONTIGNAC: (*Entering from the right.*) Monsieur Marcandier!

MARCANDIER: (*Aside.*) He's in ruddy good health, confound him; he's as healthy as a horse! But I must be patient! (*Aloud.*) Dear Monsieur Frontignac, I trust I am not calling at an inopportune moment?

FRONTIGNAC: Well, I **was** just about to go out as it happens, but I'm not in any particular hurry.

MARCANDIER: I've come to bring you this quarter's rental income.

FRONTIGNAC: As accurate as a creditor!

MARCANDIER: I've been irreproachable for the past ten years.

FRONTIGNAC: Being irreproachable is indeed a fine thing.

MARCANDIER: In five years' time, I'll begin to run at a loss, and in ten, I shall be ruined!

FRONTIGNAC: (*Incredulously.*) Oh! Oh!

MARCANDIER: That's exactly the truth of the matter.

FRONTIGNAC: Well then, there's only one thing left for it as far as I can see: you need to hope for my imminent demise!

MARCANDIER: Is that justice?

FRONTIGNAC: Only too just! You see things in a positive light, Monsieur Marcandier.

MARCANDIER: It's from a lifetime's habit of doing business. No matter, I shall remember this madness of mine for a long time to come.

FRONTIGNAC: (*Aside.*) Oh! An idea! But yes! Why didn't I think of it immediately! (*Aloud.*) So, you now regret the contract you and I entered into, Monsieur Marcandier?

MARCANDIER: Oh yes!

FRONTIGNAC: So, suppose I was to suggest … releasing you from its terms?

MARCANDIER: What? What are you talking about?

FRONTIGNAC: Does that suit you?

MARCANDIER: Well might he ask! But look here, you wretched …

FRONTIGNAC: Here's the thing: I absolutely need to get my hands on some money, quickly: and in cash.

MARCANDIER: (*Aside.*) Ah! He absolutely …

FRONTIGNAC: So that, if it's agreeable to you, you shall give me back my capital investment, and I shall release you from your obligations to pay me a private annuity.

MARCANDIER: Oh! Oh! You're quite an operator! Your 300,000 francs … but that's a fool's deal you're offering me there!

FRONTIGNAC: From my point of view, it **is**, I know that only too well!

MARCANDIER: From your point of view! You enjoy your little jokes, don't you? You know you don't look very well these days, my dear Sir?

FRONTIGNAC: What?!

MARCANDIER: Any day now, and I can have high hopes of ….

FRONTIGNAC: Will you be quiet, dash it! Do you imagine it's a cause for rejoicing, what you're telling me ...

MARCANDIER: The thing is, when all is said and done, it is certain that our contract has been in existence for the past ten years, and that, consequently, you are now ten years older than the day you signed it.

FRONTIGNAC: So, you're refusing my offer?

MARCANDIER: That's not what I said. (*Aside.*) He's in absolute need ... (*Aloud.*) The only thing is, it's only fair that there should be some negotiation of a reduction in the price.

FRONTIGNAC: How much of a reduction?

MARCANDIER: Two hundred, instead of three hundred; is that agreeable to you?

FRONTIGNAC: Two hundred; whatever!

MARCANDIER: (*Aside.*) He was very quick to accept! I've offered him too much; but what does it matter, with an iron constitution like his, I'm carrying too much risk!

FRONTIGNAC: So that's agreed, then. What do we have to do now?

MARCANDIER: We're going to draw up a provisional written agreement right here and now.

FRONTIGNAC: (*Standing up.*) He's got pens and paper there with him!

SCENE IX

THE SAME; then DOMINIQUE.

FRONTIGNAC: (*Aside.*) So it's a done deal; this is going to change my lifestyle somewhat, but what of it! Savinien is a good fellow!

DOMINIQUE: (*Coming on stage, behaving mysteriously.*) Sir!

FRONTIGNAC: (*In a low voice.*) What is it, Dominique? What's the matter?

DOMINIQUE: A woman! In the blue boudoir!

FRONTIGNAC: A blonde!

DOMINIQUE: A stranger!

FRONTIGNAC: (*To Marcandier.*) I say, my dear fellow, why don't you go on in to my library, you'll be more comfortable there. Will this take long?

MARCANDIER: Damnation!

FRONTIGNAC: Very well, I shall join you there. You, Dominique, please take our good friend Monsieur Marcandier to the library and settle him comfortably there. (*In a low voice.*) And what's more, I'm not fit to receive anyone!

DOMINIQUE: (*In a low voice.*) Understood. (*Aside.*) My master had undergone some sort of temporary personality transformation a short while ago, but it looks as though I've now got him back. (*He exits stage right, with Marcandier. Antonia enters stage left.*)

SCENE X

FRONTIGNAC, ANTONIA.

ANTONIA: Sir!

FRONTIGNAC: Ah! Here you are, at my home! How grateful I am to you!

ANTONIA: Don't start thanking me before you know why I'm here.

FRONTIGNAC: Say nothing to me, there is nothing I wish to know. You are here, I have the joy of gazing upon you, and of saying to you: I love you. What more could I possibly ask for?

ANTONIA: And yet, an undertaking of that nature …

FRONTIGNAC: I shall never forget this! I had said to myself that she would, in the end, be touched by my love!

ANTONIA: Before anything else, you must promise me …

FRONTIGNAC: Oh, the mystery of it all! Oh, Madame, with all my heart, I am so happy!

ANTONIA: Sir, such a speech! You are singularly mistaken as to the purpose of this visit. Please be good enough to hear me out.

FRONTIGNAC: Speak, my dear lady!

ANTONIA: I accept that I may have been somewhat facetious towards you … And for that, I reproach myself.

FRONTIGNAC: You are the only one who reproaches yourself, Madame, for, as far as I'm concerned …

ANTONIA: I wrote to you.

FRONTIGNAC: One letter, Madame, one single letter! In which you enclosed twenty-five concert tickets. (*Aside.*) 500 francs!

ANTONIA: Precisely. A perfectly innocent letter.

FRONTIGNAC: Too innocent!

ANTONIA: Yet it did contain a postscript which could put me in a rather compromising situation, were it to come into Roquamor's possession. My husband is jealous, suspicious. I'm convinced that he's watching me, spying upon me.

FRONTIGNAC: Eh! What? He insults you in such a manner, and you would not be revenged upon him! Oh! Pray do not withdraw that lovely hand, that first page of a book through which it is so delightful to leaf!

ANTONIA: Don't leaf through it, Sir, I beg of you … The thing is; that letter … I've come to ask for it back.

FRONTIGNAC: Never, Madame, never! (*Aside.*) This costs me quite dearly!

ANTONIA: It is a chivalrous gentleman to whom I speak.

FRONTIGNAC: And you imagine you've said it all when you have said that. That letter which bears the mark of my kisses, that letter which I reread every day … (*Aside.*) Where the devil can I have stuffed it away? (*Aloud.*) That letter, my only source of consolation in my solitary existence, my blood, my life, you have the temerity to ask me to give it back to you?

ANTONIA: Be calm!

FRONTIGNAC: Antonia!

ANTONIA: Sir!

FRONTIGNAC: I had said to myself: one day, she will take pity on this man who asks nothing of her, for indeed I ask nothing of you … (*He kisses her*)… pity on this timorous love, on this silent devotion. (*He kisses her.*) And now you come along and ask for your letter to be returned to you. (*Aside.*) I'll be damned if I know where it is.

ANTONIA: Stanislas!

FRONTIGNAC: Antonia! (*He falls to his knees.*)

ROQUAMOR: (*From outside.*) I'm coming in, I tell you!

ANTONIA: My husband's voice!

FRONTIGNAC: (*Standing up.*) It is he? By Jove, haven't I heard tell that he's a fierce character?

ANTONIA: He must have followed me. I am doomed!

FRONTIGNAC: Ah! The devil confound it!

ANTONIA: Wait … that's it! I've got an idea! Just remain calm, and back up my story when I speak …

SCENE XI

THE SAME; ROQUAMOR.

ROQUAMOR: (*Appearing to the rear.*) Aha! So I hadn't been mistaken at all, it would seem!

ANTONIA: (*To Frontignac.*) I shall ask you only whether the chimneys are smoking or not.

FRONTIGNAC: The chimneys, you say?

ROQUAMOR: (*Aside.*) The chimneys! (*Aloud.*) Madame …

ANTONIA: (*Feigning astonishment.*) It is you! What a fortunate encounter!

FRONTIGNAC: (*Aside.*) What is she talking about?

ROQUAMOR: What …?

ANTONIA: I need to ask your opinion about something.

ROQUAMOR: My opinion! When I find you here in this place, I think my opinion is rather clear.

ANTONIA: Well, the thing is, I'm viewing this apartment, it's available for rent, and since we're about to move house …

FRONTIGNAC: (*Aside.*) What? For rent! (*In a low voice.*) But … but … please allow me …

ANTONIA: Will you just act normally, and follow along with what I say; do you want to be the ruin of me?

FRONTIGNAC: No, but …

ROQUAMOR: (*Suspiciously.*) Ah! This apartment is available for rent, and that's the reason you …

ANTONIA: (*Speaking ingenuously.*) And why else do you think I would be here, my friend?

FRONTIGNAC: That's right! Why else would you expect her … (*Aside.*) Very good, Antonia!

ROQUAMOR: So, this apartment is …

ANTONIA: A most charming one: eight windows looking out onto the street; eight, isn't that so?

FRONTIGNAC: Indeed, eight.

ANTONIA: There is no type of room that isn't available here; a large and a small living room, a boudoir, a library, three bedrooms, a toilet; isn't that right?

FRONTIGNAC: A toilet … yes, perfectly correct … and others…

ANTONIA: Two cellars, isn't that right?

FRONTIGNAC: Two; perfectly correct. Ah! I say, we're going to view the cellars now, yes?

ROQUAMOR: There's no need; I am already familiar with them. I know the apartment, I know its owner.

FRONTIGNAC: Carbonnel, my friend Carbonnel.

ROQUAMOR: Our friend Carbonnel; but I also know the price.

FRONTIGNAC: Ah! That's right, five thousand francs!

ANTONIA: Which Monsieur Frontignac has reduced to two thousand until the expiry of his lease.

FRONTIGNAC: Eh?

ANTONIA: Since he finds himself forced to move from here.

ROQUAMOR: Ah! So you would be prepared to reduce the rent to two thousand?

FRONTIGNAC: Me? I … (*Aside.*) Ah! You're going too far now, Antonia.

ROQUAMOR: Well, in that case … this suits me perfectly!

FRONTIGNAC: The only thing is … ah! The only thing I mustn't try to conceal from you is that the chimneys **do** tend to be rather smoky.

ROQUAMOR: A trifling detail!

ANTONIA: A trifling detail!

FRONTIGNAC: (*Disconcerted.*) A trifling detail? Confound it! My God! After all… a trifle. (*Aside.*) Ah! But you have gone much too far, Antonia. (*Marcandier returns.*)

SCENE XII

THE SAME; MARCANDIER.

ROQUAMOR: By the way, how come you have to leave this apartment?

FRONTIGNAC: I'm obliged to … I'm obliged and yet I'm not obliged. I still haven't fully decided, to tell you the truth.

ROQUAMOR: (*Suspiciously.*) But then …

ANTONIA: Impossible! Since you are suffering from ill health.

FRONTIGNAC: I am …

ANTONIA: (*In a low voice.*) He would kill me if he knew the truth!

ROQUAMOR: You are ill?

FRONTIGNAC: Alas!

MARCANDIER: (*Aside.*) What's all this, then?

FRONTIGNAC: Dangerously ill!

ANTONIA: His chest, his bronchial tubes! It is high time that he went to breathe the pure air of the French Riviera.

MARCANDIER: He was about to take me to the cleaners!

FRONTIGNAC: (*Suffocating.*) But … but … by George …

ANTONIA: (*In a low voice.*) Start coughing, he's starting to smell a rat! Oh! Cough, damn you, cough!

FRONTIGNAC: I'm … Ah! (*He coughs.*)

ANTONIA: There you are! See!

ROQUAMOR: Poor Monsieur Frontignac!

MARCANDIER: (*Aside, slipping away.*) I can hear the violins starting up …

ANTONIA: A glass of water!

ROQUAMOR: (*Clapping him on the back.*) Some orange-flower water!

FRONTIGNAC: (*Aside.*) I'm actually coughing for real … spluttering with anger … I'm smothering … I'm suffocating.

(*The curtain falls.*)

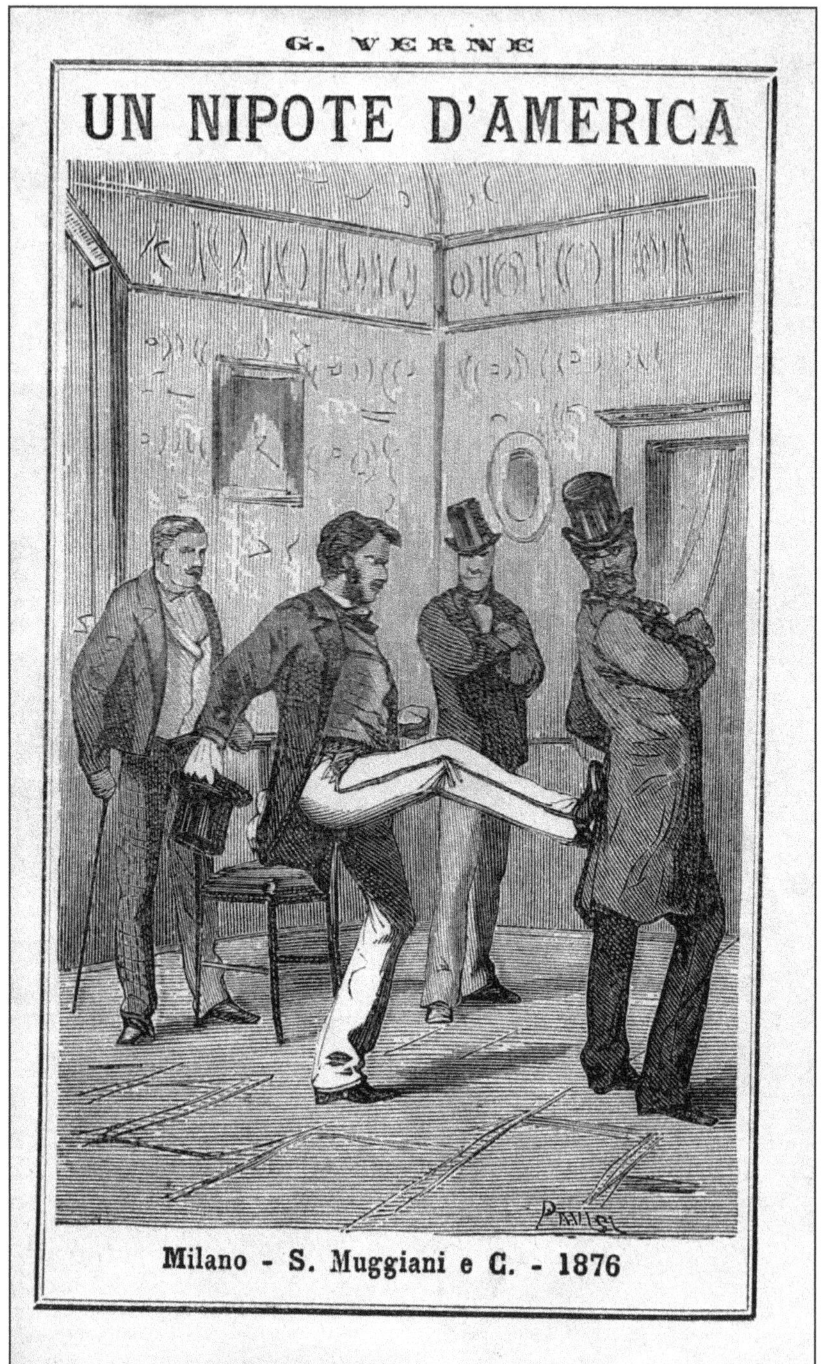

Another cover of the 19th century Italian translation.

ACT THREE

The same stage set as in the second act.

SCENE I

DOMINIQUE, *alone, then* SAVINIEN.

DOMINIQUE: How drastically he's changed in the space of a single week, my poor master; it's positively improper and indecent! All he ever talks about these days is family life, peace and quiet, an orderly existence. It makes me feel so ashamed. I do so wish I could just leave his employment! I wish I had enough hundred-centime coins to be able to give him a week's notice. Oh! Great! Here comes the other fellow!

SAVINIEN: (*Entering on stage.*) My uncle? Where's my uncle?

DOMINIQUE: He must be in the middle of saying his Pater Nosters; I'll go get him. (*He exits.*)

SAVINIEN: (*Alone.*) That poor Madame Roquamor, she has really moved me. "I will do anything you ask of me," she told me, "but you must get that letter for me. Oh! That letter!" She had tears in her eyes.

Confound it, I showered her with consolatory kisses, inasmuch as I could. A truly worthy creature, that poor lady.

SCENE II

SAVINIEN, FRONTIGNAC.

FRONTIGNAC: Ah! There you are, my lad.

SAVINIEN: Uncle, Madame Roquamor is outside with the doorman; she has begged me to bring back her letter to her, and she doesn't dare come and request it of you herself.

FRONTIGNAC: She doesn't dare? God be praised! That means we can be left in peace! As for that letter of hers, I've no doubt burnt it at this stage.

SAVINIEN: But …

FRONTIGNAC: No buts! Nothing at all! She makes me positively shudder, that woman! I have no desire to see her. I have no desire to talk about her, no desire to even think about her. She is with the doorman, you tell me? Ah! Isn't he the lucky fellow, that doorman! He doesn't realise how much he's going to enjoy himself in a short time from now. The husband must be spying on her at the corner of the street as we speak. I bet you she's forcing the doorman to change his abode too!

SAVINIEN: Ah! Well, I know, that's the thing, you see, Uncle …

FRONTIGNAC: No, you don't know, you can never know! I beg you, never speak to me about Madame Roquamor!

SAVINIEN: I have to tell you that, essentially, it makes absolutely no difference whatsoever to me.

FRONTIGNAC: In that case, not a word more about this matter, and tell me, while we're on the subject, how is your romance progressing?

SAVINIEN: It's going well, apart from the fact that Monsieur Carbonnel has thrown me out of his home, and since last week I haven't been able to exchange a single word with Madeleine.

FRONTIGNAC: Well, here's the thing: I've been corresponding with her on your behalf. Take a look at this! (*He goes to the window at the rear of the stage and catches hold of a ball of wool which is hanging from the end of a long piece of thread.*)

SAVINIEN: What's that?

FRONTIGNAC: Let's just call it my own little pony express. (*Letting out an exclamation.*) Ah!

SAVINIEN: What's the matter?

FRONTIGNAC: I just knew it, look, there at the street corner. Don't you recognize him? It's Roquamor! He's spying!

SAVINIEN: Well, then, let's not think any more about that. Come now, Uncle, you said it yourself: I don't want to think about Madame Roquamor anymore.

FRONTIGNAC: It's not she I'm thinking of: I'm thinking of the doorman. Ah! How much fun he's about to have shortly!

SAVINIEN: Well, good for him, good for him! But this pony express mail you're talking about! What on earth is that? I don't understand.

FRONTIGNAC: Well! Yesterday, at this very window, I was in a melancholy frame of mind as I sat smoking one of your excellent cigars, dwelling on a certain grey hair which, only that very morning, Dominique believed he had discovered on my left temple, when suddenly, I heard somebody uttering a slight cry. I looked up and noticed Madeleine, who had just dropped a ball of wool from her window above mine. I caught the said ball of wool in its fall, and hastily wrote, on a piece of paper: "Mademoiselle, my nephew is wasting away for love of you; if you do not give him an answer … well, I know him, he is the sort of man to blow his brains out." I tied the love letter to the ball of wool, made her a sign, the thread to which it attached was raised upwards to her, taking your declaration of love with it. A moment later it came back down again, carrying the reply… Hold on, there it is! (*He hands him a letter which he has taken out of his pocket.*) "Let Monsieur Savinien **not** blow his brains or anything else out for that matter: I love him, and I shall never love anyone else but him." Isn't that charming? What?!

SAVINIEN: (*Kissing the letter.*) Dear Madeleine!

FRONTIGNAC: After that, it was quite clear how I needed to proceed. Since yesterday, we've been exchanging a thousand declarations of undying love, each one more inflamed with passion than the previous one … inflammatory enough to have to call the Fire Brigade … Look, if you want to become intoxicated from her spidery scrawls of handwriting, here you are! You villain, here you are! (*He gives him a bundle of letters.*)

SAVINIEN: (*Kissing the letters in a transport of joy.*) What utter bliss!

FRONTIGNAC: (*Gazing at him.*) Oh! Youth! Youth! How beautiful it is! And so easily pleased! There has never been and never will be, any greater invention.

SAVINIEN: Oh! Uncle! What if I myself were to …?

FRONTIGNAC: Perfectly in order! Write to her, Savinien, and be loving, warm and eloquent.

SAVINIEN: (*After he has written his letter.*) I've finished.

FRONTIGNAC: You **have** told her: I love you?

SAVINIEN: Three times.

FRONTIGNAC: Very good! And that her uncle is a tyrant?

SAVINIEN: Constantly.

FRONTIGNAC: Very well, then. (*He ties the letter to the ball of wool and begins to hum a tune.*) "In a dark courtyard …"

SAVINIEN: What's that you're singing?

FRONTIGNAC: That's our signal! Watch, you'll see! (*The ball of wool rises.*) There it goes, now. Let's wait for the reply!

SAVINIEN: (*Taking his uncle's hand in his.*) Ah! My dear uncle! What a good idea of mine it was to come and find you.

FRONTIGNAC: You have found me! And I've found you, too.

SAVINIEN: If I had to sacrifice, today, the one I love, I do declare that I'd do something rash.

FRONTIGNAC: What rash thing do you mean?

SAVINIEN: Something risky but decisive.

FRONTIGNAC: No need; here comes the reply. Ah! Allow me … (*He takes the note which has been tied to the ball of wool.*) Let's have a look! Let us sample them, let us savor them, Savinien, let us savor these words, my friend!

SAVINIEN: You do me great honor.

FRONTIGNAC: (*Sniffing the note.*) What a delightful scent! Have a sniff of that, it's positively fragrant.

SAVINIEN: Uncle! You shall be the death of me!

FRONTIGNAC: Well then, let's read it! (*He begins to read, aloud.*) "I've figured out who you are, sonny." Hmm, she **does** seem to be addressing you rather informally. "You tacky old Don Juan." What!

SAVINIEN: What?

FRONTIGNAC: "But you can't fool a clever old fox like your good friend … Carbonnel." Ah! That old rogue! We've been caught in the act, my poor Savinien, what can we do! We've been simply caught in the act! (*He sniffs the letter and grimaces with disgust.*) What a deceptive thing it is, olfactory illusion! This smells of stale tobacco.

SAVINIEN: What should we do now?

FRONTIGNAC: I do declare, I've run clean out of ideas.

SAVINIEN: In that case, there's nothing else for it … we shall have to resort to drastic measures.

FRONTIGNAC: What kind of drastic measures do you mean?

SAVINIEN: (*To himself.*) There's only one thing for it now, more's the pity!

FRONTIGNAC: What one thing would that be?

CARBONNEL'S voice. (*Offstage.*) Where is he, that old practical joker?

FRONTIGNAC: Carbonnel.

SAVINIEN: No more hesitation; you keep him distracted a minute, but keep him well-distracted, mind! (*He exits the stage extremely hurriedly, in a wild haste.*)

FRONTIGNAC: What on earth has gotten into him?

SCENE III

FRONTIGNAC, CARBONNEL.

CARBONNEL: (*Speaking good-humoredly.*) Ah, well, there you are, you old prankster! Constantly getting up to all kinds of mischief. You're never going to take a break from getting into all sorts of mischievous scrapes. You latest trick seems to involve throwing declarations of love out through windows and inventing electric pieces of string.

FRONTIGNAC: My dear friend, I can assure you that this is all being done with the most honorable of intentions. You can't begin to imagine how many honorable intentions we have!

CARBONNEL: You really do seem to take me for some kind of incompetent, playacting guardian of Madeleine, some sort of gingerbread man …

FRONTIGNAC: (*Uttering a loud exclamation.*) A gingerbread man! My old friend, how hard you are being on me!

CARBONNEL: And all this because your nephew has returned from America. In times gone by, it used to be uncles who came back from those places, rolling in money.

FRONTIGNAC: Well, alright then, yes, I accept that I was wrong … not to succeed in my plan. But what do you expect? I've had enough of all of these diabolical machinations and manipulations which are causing such upheaval in my life and upsetting my stomach. This has got to stop; it is essential that Savinien marries Madeleine.

CARBONNEL: (*Coldly.*) That is my opinion of the matter, too.

FRONTIGNAC: (*Astonished.*) What? What are you saying?

CARBONNEL: I'm saying that that is also **my** opinion!

FRONTIGNAC: But in that case, it's all settled, then! And here was me thinking that my old friend Carbonnel had undergone a change of personality … And now I've got him back, that excellent fellow Carbonnel. So when shall the nuptials take place?

CARBONNEL: Oh! Not so fast, I have to set out my conditions first.

FRONTIGNAC: Quite right, only too right. Let's see the conditions, then.

CARBONNEL: Does your nephew possess anything other than the 1,800 francs from his office?

FRONTIGNAC: Yes.

CARBONNEL: And what might that be?

FRONTIGNAC: He has my blessing.

CARBONNEL: Do you hope to disentangle yourself from your business arrangement with Marcandier?

FRONTIGNAC: Oh, yes!

CARBONNEL: When?

FRONTIGNAC: Upon my death!

CARBONNEL: Let's continue.

FRONTIGNAC: So far, the conditions seem quite easy to me.

CARBONNEL: Frontignac!

FRONTIGNAC: My good Carbonnel!

CARBONNEL: Are you familiar with life insurance policies?

FRONTIGNAC: By reputation; they must make people die young.

CARBONNEL: On the contrary, they allow one to live to a ripe old age! So listen carefully. I've already told you, and let me repeat, that Madeleine has little in the way of personal fortune, so it's absolutely necessary that your nephew should have, if not assets already in his possession, then at least a reasonable expectancy of acquiring same.

FRONTIGNAC: Expectancy! You couldn't have chosen a funnier term!

CARBONNEL: Well, a life insurance policy paid out in the case of death, gives you the means of fulfilling the condition. Think about it; follow my line of reasoning.

FRONTIGNAC: Willingly, but I do beg you, don't be saying too much about my demise; I find it a rather distasteful subject.

CARBONNEL: What are you due to receive from Marcandier? Ten per cent of the sum he has taken as a life annuity, thirty thousand francs. Well, take away two per cent of that, six thousand francs from that income, and use them to pay an annual policy to my own company which, on the day you pass on to your eternal reward—see how I'm looking after your interests—will have two hundred thousand francs for your nephew Savinien.

FRONTIGNAC: Well well, I say! But that's extremely clever of you! But are you really sure that this won't bring me ill fortune?

CARBONNEL: On the contrary! As the company pays out only when the insured person dies, it's completely in its own interest to prolong his life, it watches over him or her, it protects him like a tender mother; all those centenarians whose names you see published in the newspapers are clients of ours. I would even wager you that, back in the day, the late Methusaleh himself ... there can hardly be any other way to explain his extraordinarily long life.

FRONTIGNAC: Come on now, don't be talking nonsense, are you really sure about all this?

CARBONNEL: Am I not the managing director of the ***Lutetian***?

FRONTIGNAC: Well, that **is** true…

CARBONNEL: Well, then, you see! Does the condition meet with your agreement, then?

FRONTIGNAC: (*Hesitantly.*) Do you have a life insurance policy of your own?

CARBONNEL: But of course!

FRONTIGNAC: But in that case, how come I don't have a life insurance policy too?

CARBONNEL: Because you're nothing but a silly goose!

FRONTIGNAC: (*Taking offence.*) Carbonnel!

CARBONNEL: Well, then … a selfish man.

FRONTIGNAC: Marvellous!

CARBONNEL: So, it's settled then; this is acceptable to you?

FRONTIGNAC: Perfectly so.

CARBONNEL: In that case, let me just send for the doctor.

FRONTIGNAC: A doctor, you say? Which doctor?

CARBONNEL: The official doctor used by the Company; Doctor Imbert, a charming man who will come to give you a check-up in a friendly way, listen to the sound of your chest and all that.

FRONTIGNAC: (*Suspiciously, distrustfully.*) He listens to your chest?

CARBONNEL: And taps you here and there.

FRONTIGNAC: He taps you? He'll do no such thing to me!

CARBONNEL: Why not?

FRONTIGNAC: It tickles me.

CARBONNEL: But look, think logically about this. Do you really think the life insurance company would be quite happy to give a policy to some fellow who might have only another two or three years left to live? Don't you think it necessary that they make sure his lungs are sound, his heart healthy and his stomach solid?

FRONTIGANC. And if the lungs, heart or stomach left something to be desired?

CARBONNEL: The doctor wouldn't sign your medical certificate and the Company wouldn't agree to take out a policy on you, and that would be that.

FRONTIGNAC: And that would be that! It's simply ferocious! So, the client who thinks he's fit and healthy suddenly learns, there and then, quite bluntly and without any pussyfooting around the issue, that his passport for the next world has already been stamped? Hmpph!

CARBONNEL: Dash and confound it, man, what do you expect? No medical certificate, no deal.

FRONTIGNAC: But that's awful, that is! It's horrifying! Just thinking about it gives me goose bumps. I don't want to see that doctor of yours. To hell with your doctor!

CARBONNEL: Come on now! Should this be any concern to you, a fine strapping fellow like you? What's more, as I've already told you, my dear fellow, it's an essential formality, and also …

FRONTIGNAC: Enough! You mean there are **two** of them now?

CARBONNEL: No! One is sufficient, but as I truly believed, in advance, that you would agree to my proposition, I have already requested Doctor Imbert to call on you.

FRONTIGNAC: You mean … he's coming here?

CARBONNEL: (*Consulting his watch.*) He's due any minute now.

FRONTIGNAC: Good grief! Couldn't you have given me a little more notice? And what about getting dressed and groomed properly in preparation for his visit?

CARBONNEL: You're grooming? But you are of such elegance that … One might almost think you were going to attend a burial!

FRONTIGNAC: (*Shaking his hand violently.*) Carbonnel!

CARBONNEL: No, no! I meant … to a wedding.

FRONTIGNAC: (*Very emotional.*) Don't make those sort of jokes please, Carbonnel: I must be as pale as a … A doctor! A doctor! (*The sound of the doorbell ringing is heard.*)

CARBONNEL: There he is! That'll be him!

FRONTIGNAC: Ask him to wait! (*Aside.*) I'm going to have to apply something to my face to make my complexion look a little rosier, ruddier, healthier. (*Aloud.*) It's all the same: a doctor! A doctor! (*He exits the stage just at the very moment that Marcandier enters from the rear.*)

SCENE IV

CARBONNEL, MARCANDIER.

MARCANDIER: (*Who has just overheard Frontignac's most recent words.*) A doctor! Frontignac is asking for a doctor, no less!

CARBONNEL: Eh! My God! Yes, dear Monsieur Marcandier, he's finally made the decision, taken the plunge and gone and gotten himself some medical help at last, but it may already be too late, alas! His state of health, damaged and compromised as it has been through long years of abuse and excess …

MARCANDIER: Could this be true?

CARBONNEL: His health, which has been most gravely compromised, requires the most stringent of treatment and medical attention…

MARCANDIER: Ah! My God!

CARBONNEL: Finally, I've successfully persuaded our mutual friend – not without some difficulty, mind you – to agree to accept a doctor's services. God willing, Doctor Imbert won't find anything wrong with him, not the trace of any serious illness or any unwanted germs …

MARCANDIER: Most serious!

CARBONNEL: If not most serious, at least …

MARCANDIER: Fatal? Deadly?

CARBONNEL: As you say.

MARCANDIER: It makes you wonder what kind of creatures we are at all… A man who appeared to enjoy such flourishing, ruddy good health …

CARBONNEL: And yet, perhaps I'm wrong to be concerned. In any event, we're soon about to find out what the true state of his health really is, for I've made an appointment with the doctor to come here to the apartment.

MARCANDIER: However prejudicial it may be towards my own ailment, will you allow me to be present at the consultation?

CARBONNEL: Knowing you as I do to be a sensitive, impressionable and easily-upset man, I think you might be better advised to …

MARCANDIER: No! No! I shall indeed have the strength to conceal my emotions. And what's more, believe me, let's not alter this sick man's lifestyle too abruptly. (*The doorbell rings.*)

CARBONNEL: Ah! This is probably the doctor.

DOMINIQUE: (*Announcing him.*) Doctor Imbert!

CARBONNEL: (*To Dominique.*) Kindly inform your master that the doctor has arrived.

MARCANDIER: (*Aside.*) At last, I'm going to find out what I'm really up against as regards his state of health!

SCENE V

CARBONNEL, MARCANDIER, IMBERT, *followed by* FRONTIGNAC.

CARBONNEL: My dear Doctor, allow me to shake your hand.

IMBERT: Eh! But, Monsieur Marcandier, I'm surely already amongst friends here in this place.

MARCANDIER: Do not conceal anything from us, Doctor, conceal nothing from us: we shall be courageous enough to cope with whatever we have to hear from you. (*Seeing Frontignac enter stage right.*) Sssh! (*Frontignac greets the doctor in a rather forced, tense manner.*)

CARBONNEL: (*Introducing them to each other.*) M. de Frontignac; Doctor Imbert.

FRONTIGNAC: Monsieur!

IMBERT: Sir, you are aware of why I am here today. I hope that I shall have nothing to convey to you but favorable diagnoses.

FRONTIGNAC: (*Aside.*) He's polite, I'll give him that, but will he sign that certificate of his? (*Calling.*) Dominique!

CARBONNEL: What is it you want?

FRONTIGNAC: A pen and some ink for the doctor's certificate.

CARBONNEL: (*Pointing out the table to him.*) Everything necessary is already in place, there on that table.

IMBERT: (*Smiling.*) You are in a hurry, Sir?

FRONTIGNAC: I'm due to meet somebody.

MARCANDIER: (*Aside.*) The fact is, he has an unhealthy complexion.

IMBERT: If you will be good enough to be seated.

FRONTIGNAC: (*Sitting down to the side of the stage, and speaking in an aside.*) Does he have his medical equipment with him? Ah! Savinien, Savinien! You'll never realize how much you are costing me!

IMBERT: Hold still.

FRONTIGNAC: (*Aside.*) He's a photographer! (*Imbert listens to Frontignac's back.*) Come in!

IMBERT: Now, I want you to inhale loudly and deeply. (*Frontignac breathes till he's ready to burst.*)

MARCANDIER: (*Aside.*) Hold on a minute; suppose I, too, were to undergo a medical examination! (*He imitates Frontignac, but breathes with difficulty.*)

IMBERT: Now say: ba, beh, bi, bo, bu.

FRONTIGNAC: What?

CARBONNEL: Say: ba.

FRONTIGNAC: (*Aside.*) This cannot be; he's a schoolmaster now, it seems! (*Speaking forcefully.*) Ba, beh, bi, bo, bu.

MARCANDIER: (*Weakly.*) Ba, be, bi, bo, bu.

IMBERT: (*Shifting his glance from Marcandier to Frontignac in turn.*) Ah!

FRONTIGNAC: (*Standing up, he goes to the table, takes a pen and offers it to Imbert.*) Doctor!

IMBERT: What's that?

FRONTIGNAC: A pen … to sign the certificate with.

IMBERT: Oh! But we haven't yet finished. Sit down again, and this time, I want you to cough.

FRONTIGNAC: (*Sitting down.*) What—you want me to cough?

MARCANDIER: You're being asked to cough, it's not all that hard you know; as for me, I cough whenever I wish to.

FRONTIGNAC: And even when you don't wish to. (*Aside.*) Savinien! Savinien!

MARCANDIER: (*Coughing.*) Hum!

IMBERT: (*Mistakenly thinking that it is Frontignac who has just coughed.*) Oh dear! That's a nasty cough!

MARCANDIER: What! A nasty cough … but …

FRONTIGNAC: (*Coughing like the sound of a roll of thunder.*) Ahem!

IMBERT: Now that's what I call a cough and a half! How hollow it sounds, how soft! A burst of cannon fire!

FRONTIGNAC: Has the performance ended?

IMBERT: One moment more. (*He begins to punch him in the back.*)

FRONTIGNAC: Good heavens! Now he's a boxing instructor!

IMBERT: What effect does that have on you?

FRONTIGNAC: (*Radiant.*) I feel nothing at all.

MARCANDIER: (*Beating his own chest.*) It makes **me** feel pain!

FRONTIGNAC: (*Standing up and handing the pen to Imbert.*) Doctor, the pen …

IMBERT: A few questions and we're done. In the mornings, at around eleven o'clock or thereabouts, do you happen to feel any sharp pains in your stomach?

FRONTIGNAC: (*Keeping the pen in his hand.*) Yes, I do, actually.

MARCANDIER: (*Aside.*) Me too!

IMBERT: And at about ten o'clock in the evening, don't those stomach pains flare up again?

FRONTIGNAC: (*Worriedly.*) They **do** start up again, actually.

MARCANDIER: (*Aside.*) Same for me!

IMBERT: And towards midnight, do you not begin to feel a certain heaviness in your eyebrows, desires to yawn, feelings of drowsiness and sleepiness?

FRONTIGANC. (*Feeling more and more ill-at-ease and now concealing the pen he had been holding in his hand.*) I do indeed have all those symptoms.

MARCANDIER: (*Aside.*) Just as I do!

IMBERT: Whenever you've just done a strenuous bout of physical exercise, do you not feel a certain weariness in your joints and the need to sit down?

FRONTIGNAC: (*Looking at his pen with a shamefaced, pitiful demeanour.*) I feel all that!

MARCANDIER: (*Aside.*) Me too!

IMBERT: I'll just run quickly through the other symptoms: the desire to warm yourself up whenever the weather is cold, to seek out cool air when the weather is warm …

FRONTIGNAC: Yes, yes!

MARCANDIER: Yes, yes!

IMBERT: Ah! Ah!

FRONTIGNAC: So … is it very serious, Doctor? Let's not prolong the agony a moment more… (*He makes to snap the pen in two, when Imbert takes it from him and goes back upstage.*)

IMBERT: Well, my good man, as long as you don't fall from the fifth storey of some high building; as long as you don't jump into a steamboat or railway train, don't get struck on the head by a falling chimney or impaled by a spike which runs right through your body, you stand a strong chance of outliving us all, seeing us all out of town as it were: you'll live a hundred years. (*As he utters those last few words, Imbert, all the while fiddling with the pen, has taken from his wallet a sheet of paper, signed it, and handed it to Frontignac.*) There's your medical certificate, Sir.

FRONTIGNAC: (*Who has been anxiously following all the intricacies of the last scene, and upon witnessing its resolution, utters a very loud exclamation of joy.*) Hum!

IMBERT: Oh! It's pointless getting emotional at this stage.

MARCANDIER: A hundred years! (*Going up to Carbonnel.*) Well, what about that, then? But what was it you'd told me?

CARBONNEL: It appears I was mistaken. Let us rejoice!

FRONTIGNAC: A hundred years! Ah! Doctor, how lovely it is to hear that news! And I who used to hate doctors … A hundred years! Are you not exaggerating? … A little … come now …

IMBERT: (*Laughing.*) Well … perhaps by an hour or two.

FRONTIGNAC: You are the King of Physicians! You shall henceforth be my friend, my companion! You shall nevermore leave my side!

MARCANDIER: (*Aside.*) This man is being positively cynical in waxing lyrically on about his wretched old health!

IMBERT: (*Making his goodbyes and leaving, upstage.*) Sir! (*To the others.*) Gentlemen!

FRONTIGNAC: Delighted, Doctor, to have made your acquaintance. (*He follows him upstage to show him out.*)

SCENE VI

CARBONNEL, MARCANDIER.

MARCANDIER: Will you kindly explain to me, Monsieur Carbonnel, what that was all about? What is the meaning of this little scene I have just witnessed?

CARBONNEL: Nothing could be simpler, my dear fellow. Our friend Frontignac, having grown weary of your procrastination, and desirous of bequeathing a lump sum to his nephew, has just had a sum of 200,000 francs insured at ***The Lutetian.***

MARCANDIER: (*Aside.*) **I've** been had!

SCENE VII

THE SAME CHARACTERS; FRONTIGNAC.

FRONTIGNAC: (*Returning.*) You know something, that doctor of yours is a positively charming fellow.

CARBONNEL: What did I tell you? (*He takes a paper from his pocket.*) Now, if you'll just sign this piece of paper for me, and I'll have the contract drawn up and get it to you within the hour.

FRONTIGANC. As you wish.

CARBONNEL: Come along, Monsieur Marcandier.

MARCANDIER: (*Aside.*) Ah! I've just been made a complete fool of! Well, just wait till the opportunity arises, and I'll show them …!

FRONTIGNAC: Goodbye, goodbye! (*He shows them out.*)

SCENE VIII

FRONTIGNAC: (*alone*) People are wrong to be so harshly critical of doctors; they are indispensable … when you aren't ill. That's Savinien's future guaranteed. It's true, of course, that, because of this scheme, I'm going to lose one-fifth of my revenue; but, as for that, truly, I have no regrets at all! He marries Madeleine, and within a year gives me half a dozen grand-nephews … well, half a dozen is perhaps being quite ambitious for just one year; but still, he **is** an American! (*Antonia enters.*) What matter! I'm sorted out and I'm easy in my mind. I've cut myself off forever from my former existence, living the high life and having banal adventures and love affairs. This feels delightful!

SCENE IX

FRONTIGNAC, ANTONIA.

ANTONIA: Good day, Monsieur de Frontignac.

FRONTIGNAC: Madame Roquamor! My God, but what a fright you've given me!

ANTONIA: (*In a flirtatious, coquettish manner.*) Ah, but come now! Wouldn't anybody think that my presence was bothering you?

FRONTIGNAC: Your presence, bothering me? Horribly!

ANTONIA: What …?

FRONTIGNAC: You weren't really with the doorman, then?

ANTONIA: But …

FRONTIGNAC: But you don't know, then, that your husband, that vulture, that jackal of a husband of yours, is at the corner of the street spying on you as we speak; and if he were to come here right now, I wouldn't be long about settling his hash!

ANTONIA: Sir …

FRONTIGNAC: You again … Oh! You, yes, always **you,** because, **you,** at the end of the day …

ANTONIA: I, Sir, am infinitely mortified by your manner of receiving me just now. Using the excuse of my husband is clever of you, no doubt, but unworthy of a man who had had no scruples about compromising the reputation of a poor young woman. But in the end, I have come to my senses and realized my foolish indiscretions, and it is thus my letter that I have now come to collect from you.

FRONTIGNAC: Your letter! Ah! If only I knew where the heck I put it! I must have burnt it, Madam; yes, that's it, I burnt it …

ANTONIA: (*Troubled.*) Oh! A fitting punishment indeed for my moment of flirtatiousness. But this is unworthy of you, Sir.

FRONTIGNAC: (*Aside.*) I bet you one hundred centimes that the husband is about to show up.

ANTONIA: A poor defenceless woman is courted; recourse is had to the sweetest and mellowest of poetry in order to dazzle her; her suitor behaves as though he is in utter despair for love of her. So, this woman takes pity on him! She writes a sympathetic note to him and, in the process, unwittingly furnishes a weapon against herself. (*She falls down into a seat.*)

FRONTIGNAC: (*In a lively, animated manner.*) A weapon! What is it that you suspect me of, Madame; you think that I was just acting a part?! Oh! Such an act is unworthy of me … (*He comes closer to her.*) No, my mouth has uttered no lies whatsoever. But (*he clutches her hand in his*) I too have reflected upon the fecklessness of what we did, I too have now turned back to the path of righteousness. (*He clutches Antonia's hand in his, and continues, effusively.*) I have realized how wicked it is to deceive one's fellow man! For (*he kisses Antonia's hands*) it must not be thought for one moment that I refuse to consider your husband as one of my fellow men! (*He continues to kiss her hand.*) He is indeed my fellow man, Antonia. (*He sits down beside her.*) I swear that to you; and when I think back on all that I had said to you, on those poems, on those outpourings of sweetness, I felt ashamed of myself, for, believe me, Antonia (*he hugs her*) believe me, oh my angel! There is nothing true, in this life, but honorable intentions. (*He kisses her.*)

ANTONIA: But, Sir …

FRONTIGNAC: Don't you see how much peace is in our hearts, now that they are filled with virtue? (*He continues to kiss her.*)

ANTONIA: But … please … please!

FRONTIGNAC: What?

ANTONIA: But, you're kissing me!

FRONTIGNAC: Perfectly; with all my heart. (*He continues to indulge in the same behaviour.*)

ANTONIA: But, but …

FRONTIGNAC: And what of it? Since we all have nothing but the most honorable of intentions … (*He gets down on his knees.*)

ANTONIA: Stanislas, please, I beseech you …

FRONTIGANC: (*Passionately.*) Ah! Angel! Oh! My angel! If my voice is still capable of moving your soul, if I've managed to reawaken some echo of your former feelings for me, I beg you … go back to the doorman.

ANTONIA: (*Standing up.*) Ah!

ROQUAMOR'S VOICE: (*Coming from outside.*) My wife is in here!

ANTONIA: It's my husband!

FRONTIGNAC: What did I tell you?!

ANTONIA: I am lost … hide me!

FRONTIGNAC: (*Aside.*) She was so much better off with the doorman.

ANTONIA: Where can I flee to?

FRONTIGNAC: You can go back down outside by the back stairs. You shall forgive me if I don't personally escort you. (*Antonia runs away through the same door by which Savinien had exited in the second scene. Frontignac, still troubled, has remained seated. The door to the rear suddenly opens.*)

SCENE X

FRONTIGNAC, ROQUAMOR, MARCANDIER.

ROQUAMOR: Kneeling down! He's kneeling down? Where is she?

MARCANDIER: Under the sofa! (*He bends down.*)

FRONTIGNAC: (*Astonished.*) Monsieur Marcandier!

ROQUAMOR: What are you doing down there?

FRONTIGNAC: Penance for the error of my ways … and I'm also looking for a pin, as it happens.

ROQUAMOR: Sir, enough of all this subterfuge! My wife has been seen coming into this house!

FRONTIGNAC: Who exactly has seen her?

ROQUAMOR: That's of little consequence! She **has** to be somewhere in here. Do you dare to deny it?

MARCANDIER: (*Aside.*) Ah! My lad, you still expect to live a hundred years **now**, do you?!

ROQUAMOR: Your silence is an admission in itself. What's more, I'll find her soon enough. (*He makes his way towards the left.*)

FRONTIGNAC: (*Standing up.*) I beg your pardon, my dear Monsieur Roquamor, but you have rented my apartment, and that is all well and good! But only with effect from July 15th; so (*he positions himself in front of the door situated to the left*) that means that in three weeks' time, you will be able to check, at your leisure, whether or not Madame Roquamor is here.

ROQUAMOR: Is this some kind of joke?

FRONTIGNAC: And until then, may I remind you that a visit to another party's domestic premises must adhere to certain procedures as prescribed by law.

MARCANDIER: A commissioner!

ROQUAMOR: Now that's going too far, Sir, I'm sure you will agree.

FRONTIGNAC: Yes, Sir!

MARCANDIER: (*Aside.*) That's it!

ROQUAMOR: Let us go outside!

FRONTIGNAC: Yes, let us go outside!

SCENE XI

THE SAME CHARACTERS AS IN THE PREVIOUS SCENE; CARBONNEL.

CARBONNEL: The policy! Here's the policy!

ROQUAMOR AND FRONTIGNAC: What!

MARCANDIER: The commissioner!

ROQUAMOR: Ah! Monsieur is arranging his protection!

FRONTIGNAC: Ah! Monsieur is having himself escorted.

CARBONNEL: What are they saying? But no! I didn't say **police**, I said **policy** … the insurance policy.

FRONTIGNAC: It is indeed a question of insurance. We are fighting a duel with Monsieur, and you shall act as my second.

CARBONNEL: You are fighting a duel! But the company strictly forbids duelling!

FRONTIGNAC: Come on then!

CARBONNEL: (*Animatedly.*) Enough of your "Come on then!" Here is your contract, you have signed it and you have thus entered into a formal undertaking to live as long as you possibly can, and to never put your life in reckless danger: to fight a duel would thus be rather indiscreet. Ah! The company would do fine business indeed if its clients had the right to receive a bullet in the head or a sword in the chest; that would be just too convenient; you sign up for life insurance, you get yourself killed and someone receives one hundred thousand francs. You cannot, and you shall not!

MARCANDIER: (*Aside.*) Ah! The villain!

ROQUAMOR: (*Mockingly.*) Now that – of course! – is something that's been extremely well thought out. People are insulted, others accept the offer of a duel, and then at the last minute the company forbids you to duel, to defend your honor.

CARBONNEL: There's a subtle distinction here! The company allows him to kill you, but not to get himself killed.

FRONTIGNAC: This is nonsensical! Absurd! Monstrous! And I'm going to …

CARBONNEL: Disinherit your nephew!

FRONTIGNAC: (*Appalled.*) Good heavens!

MARCANDIER: (*Aside.*) Ah! You cannot fight a duel, you scheming rascal! (*Aloud.*) So, if it was said that you are nothing but a womanizing rogue …

FRONTIGNAC: (*Managing to contain himself.*) Monsieur Marcandier!

MARCANDIER: A bumpkin! A prig.

FRONTIGNAC: (*Still containing himself.*) Monsieur Marcandier!

MARCANDIER: A ridiculous ninny!

FRONTIGNAC: A ninny … oh! (*At the very moment that Marcandier turns away contemptuously, Frontignac administers him a kick in the behind. – To Cabonnel.*) Well, is **that** prohibited by this insurance policy of yours?

CARBONNEL: It's permitted!

MARCANDIER: Oh!

ROQUAMOR: Ah! Sir, are we going to take this outside, or are we not going to take this outside?

FRONTIGNAC: I'll be right with you. (*To Carbonnel.*) Too bad!

CARBONNEL: Well, in that case, the whole thing is null and void, and your nephew can go to Hell!

SCENE XII

THE SAME CHARACTERS AS IN THE PREVIOUS SCENE; ANTONIA.

ANTONIA: Don't say that, Monsieur Carbonnel.

ROQUAMOR: My wife!

FRONTIGNAC: (*Aside.*) The plot thickens! It's getting rather heated now …

ANTONIA: No, don't say that! He was already going there, Monsieur Carbonnel.

CARBONNEL: Going where? To Hell?

ANTONIA: Straight to Hell; but not alone; with your niece.

CARBONNEL: Madeleine …

ANTONIA: Whom he had abducted this very morning.

CARBONNEL: While I was here.

FRONTIGNAC: While you were in the process of insuring me!

CARBONNEL: But where are they now?

ANTONIA: Listen to me! After he managed to persuade Madeleine to run away with him, he brought her to your sister-in-law's home. Unfortunately, she wasn't there … They hadn't had anything to eat! What was there to do?

FRONTIGNAC: The poor children! …

CARBONNEL: Be quiet!

ANTONIA: So he took her to the Moulin Rouge.

FRONTIGNAC: (*Now rendered more docile; tenderly.*) But … that is heart-breaking to hear.

ANTONIA: There, they were served the most trifling of snacks: six dozen oysters from Ostende, some foie gras, partridge, some fruit and vegetables and a parfait cream dessert, all washed down with a thimble of champagne.

FRONTIGNAC: (*Emotionally.*) And the coffee, the liqueurs … This is driving me to tears …

CARBONNEL: And my niece dared to … there … at a restaurant table … in the middle of a crowd of pleasure-seekers …

ANTONIA: No, don't worry! They had reserved a private dining room.

CARBONNEL: A private dining room!

FRONTIGNAC: How discreet!

ANTONIA: Then, they had a coach sent for.

CARBONNEL: To take them where …?

ANTONIA: To the countryside somewhere: I spotted them at the railway station where I'd gone to collect the new housemaid who's coming to me from Normandy. Savinien was at the ticket office, and was asking for two first-class tickets to San Francisco.

MARCANDIER: (*Aside.*) So that's what she calls going "to the countryside somewhere!"

ANTONIA: I begged them, I got through to their finer sentiments and managed to convince them to come back to your place where, for three long hours, I've been waiting for you.

ROQUAMOR: (*In an outpouring of sudden regret, to Frontignac, offering him his hand to shake.*) You know, I owe you an apology, my dear fellow, my close, valued friend! (*Pointing to Marcandier.*) It is this gentleman here who had put the idea into my head …

FRONTIGNAC: At the end of the day, better inside than on top.

CARBONNEL: But what about **them** … those monsters!

ANTONIA: (*Opening the door on the left.*) There they are!

SCENE XIII

THE SAME CHARACTERS AS BEFORE; ALSO MADELEINE, SAVINIEN.

(*Madeleine is extremely red in the face, while Savinien seems somewhat hurried. He is holding a small cage, in which there is a canary. They take a few steps into the room and stop, seeming confused, like two children who have just been caught red-handed in an act of mischief. A brief silence ensues.*)

CARBONNEL: (*Taking a step towards them.*) So, Madeleine … (*Madeleine, startled, nestles into Savinien's chest and hides her face in it.*)

MADELEINE: My God!

CARBONNEL: Well!

SAVINIEN: She is trying to hide her confusion. (*He looks as though he is about to burst into tears.*) If only I could hide my own! …

CARBONNEL: And suppose I were to demand satisfaction from you?

FRONTIGNAC: You cannot do so, my friend.

CARBONNEL: What?

FRONTIGNAC: You are insured!

CARBONNEL: That's right!

FRONTIGNAC: And so, then, are they thus truly guilty? You have to look at the intentions behind an action, after all. Just a moment ago, Monsieur Roquamor suspected his wife of infidelity, and yet, she, like them, has done nothing except with … good intentions. That sums it all up, my friend: you must show kindness towards others only.

CARBONNEL: So, then, what is your view of the matter?

FRONTIGNAC: Let us give them our blessing! (*Everybody expresses agreement.*)

CARBONNEL: Let us go!

MADELEINE: Ah! My uncle!

SAVINIEN: (*To Carbonnel.*) Ah! My uncle!

FRONTIGNAC: And similarly converted as we are, we shall spend the rest of our days close by them.

MADELEINE: Well cared-for, well-loved, well-cherished.

FRONTIGNAC: In the bosom of a loving family!

MARCANDIER: (*Aside.*) In the bosom of a loving family: I am ruined! (*Curtain falls.*)

THE END

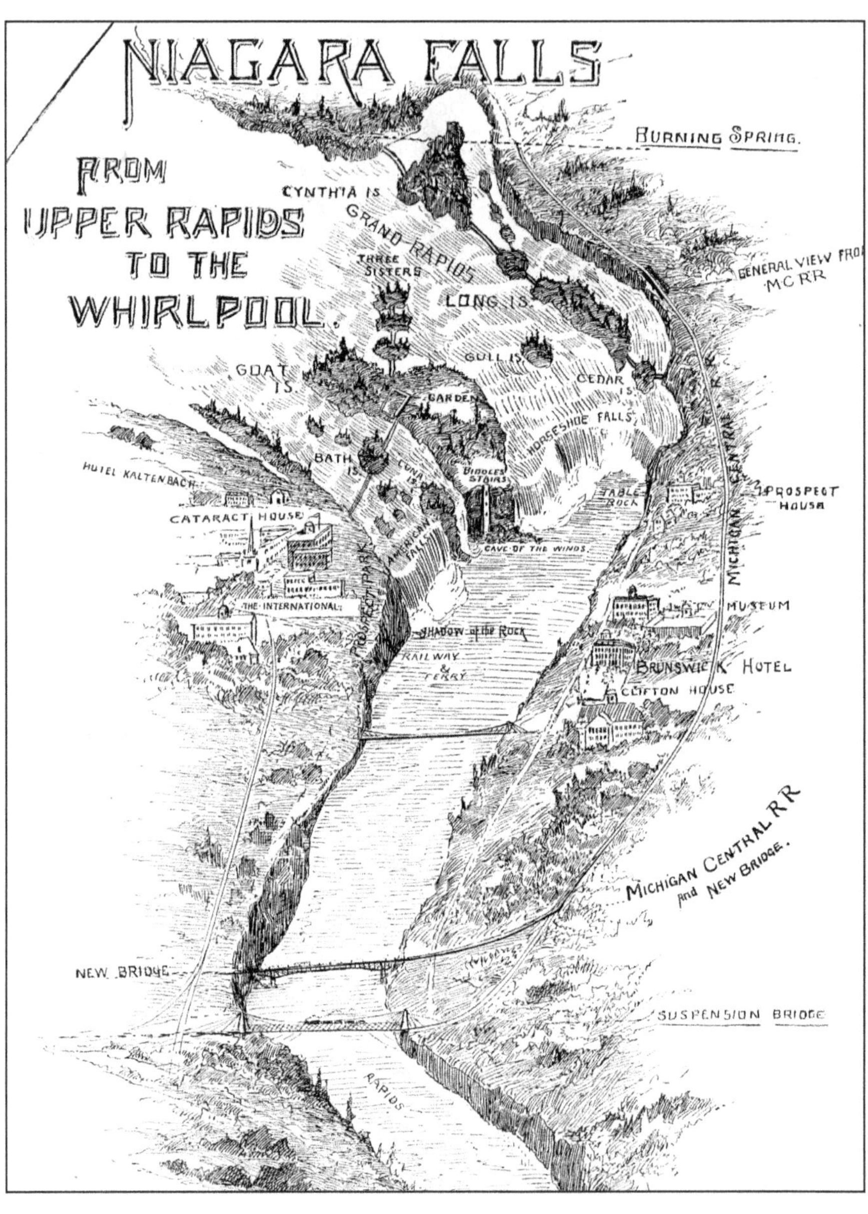
NIAGARA FALLS
FROM UPPER RAPIDS TO THE WHIRLPOOL.
BURNING SPRING.
CYNTHIA IS
GRAND RAPIDS
THREE SISTERS
LONG IS.
GENERAL VIEW FROM MCRR
GULL IS.
GOAT IS.
CEDAR IS.
GARDEN
HORSESHOE FALLS
BATH IS.
LUNA IS.
BIDDLES STAIRS
HOTEL KALTENBACH
TABLE ROCK
PROSPECT HOUSE
CATARACT HOUSE
AMERICAN FALLS
CAVE OF THE WINDS
MICHIGAN CENTRAL RR
PROSPECT PARK
THE INTERNATIONAL
MUSEUM
SHADOW of the ROCK
RAILWAY & FERRY
BRUNSWICK HOTEL
CLIFTON HOUSE
MICHIGAN CENTRAL RR And NEW BRIDGE.
NEW BRIDGE
SUSPENSION BRIDGE
RAPIDS

Appendix

Jules Verne's Trip to America

By Brian Taves

Three countries fascinated Verne above all others. One was naturally his own native France. Another was England, the most powerful nation in the world due to its farflung colonial empire, on which the sun truly never set—a nation with tendencies he both admired and deplored. Above these, however, was the United States—the heart of the new world in the 19th century and a nation symbolizing hope and the future.

Over a third of Verne's novels featured the United States, her citizens, or the American continent. The lack of tradition and the belief in individual initiative appealed to the author. The United States was the land of Yankee ingenuity, inventiveness, and industrialization, part of the technological wave that formed the undercurrent for Verne's series of novels, the "Extraordinary Journeys." The United States was also the home of the Wild West, and the American Civil War was a pivotal event in the century. Verne produced an antislavery, prounion historical novel of the conflict, *North against South* (*Nord contre Sud*, 1887), together with a novelette, *The Blockade Runners* (*Les Forceurs de blocus*, 1865). The opening and the characterizations of *The Mysterious Island* (*L'Île mystérieuse*, 1875), and *From the Earth to the Moon* (*De la Terre à la Lune*, 1865) are also indebted to his pro-

Northern sentiments. (However, Verne did support secession when it had a political commitment to freedom, and Quebec's struggle for independence from the oppression of British Canada is heroically portrayed in *Family Without a Name* [*Famille-sans*-nom, 1889].)

In turn, the United States found in Verne her own obsessions with technology, power, and freedom. However, Verne's vision of the United States was not always positive; he saw the country as a center of mechanical engineering that could be used for both good and evil, whether the hot air balloons of the Weldon Society in *Robur the Conqueror* (*Robur-le-Conqurérant*, 1886), or the astronomical exploits of the Baltimore Gun Club in *From the Earth to the Moon*, *Around the Moon* (*Autour de la Lune*, 1870), and *Topsy Turvy* (*Sans dessus dessous*, 1889). An even more dangerous engineer, Robur, centers his exploits in North America, revealing a strange affinity that obliges him to exhibit the *Terror* nowhere else, although he proclaims himself master of the world. In *Facing the Flag* (*Face au drapeau*, 1896), the weapons inventor Thomas Roch has been imprisoned by the government in a North Carolina asylum. The United States is also full of cranks, frauds, and schemers, for whom no undertaking is too audacious or extravagant, whether *The Hunt for the Meteor* (*La Chasse au météore*, 1908), the purchase of an island *School for Robinsons* (*L'École des Robinsons*, 1882), or the contest that executed *The Will of an Eccentric* (*Le Testament d'un excentrique*, 1899). As economic progress turned increasingly materialistic, giving rise to the robber barons, Verne satirized the self destructive greed of a city for millionaires on *Propeller Island* (*L'Île à hélice*, 1895).[1] The United States is not the only portion of the American continents to interest Verne; he is enchanted by the entire new world, including Latin America, from Cape Horn to Hudson Bay and the frozen north.

The sincerity of Verne's interest in the United States is demonstrated by the fact that he had already used this country as a setting for *From the Earth to the Moon* and *The Blockade Runners* before his books had been discovered by English-language readers. As well, the

1. Of all these books set in the United States, nearly all appeared in this country simultaneously with their French publication or within a reasonable time afterward; only *The Will of an Eccentric* would have to wait more than a century before its American appearance: Jules Verne, *The Will of an Eccentric*, with an afterword by Brian Taves (St. Michaels, MD: Choptank Press, 2009), designed by Norman Wolcott and sold through Lulu.com.

two plays in this volume were written before Verne became known in this country. Verne made his only journey to the United States in the spring of 1867, at a time when he was virtually unknown in the English-speaking world, although his books were already becoming best-sellers in France. Verne's second published short story, "A Balloon Journey" ("Un Voyage en Ballon," 1851) written when he was age 23, was apparently the first of his works to have been translated into English, in 1852.[2] However, the first English translation of one of his novels did not appear until the same year in which Verne came to the United States. *From the Earth to the Moon* was serialized in the *New York Weekly Magazine of Popular Literature, Science and Art*, beginning in the January 26, 1867 issue.

By this point, Jules Verne was sufficiently prosperous that he had just bought a small vessel of his own, the *Saint-Michel*, the first of Verne's three so-named ships. One factor in choosing this moment was because he could make the trip on a ship redolent of his own imaginings, on what promised to be a well-publicized, notable voyage of the world's largest and most famous ocean liner, the *Great Eastern*. Launched in 1857, the iron-hulled vessel was some 690 feet in length, with a draw of 35 feet, and driven by a 24-foot propeller, two 58-foot paddle wheels, and sails on six masts.[3] The French Emperor, Napoleon III, had conceived the idea of refitting the *Great Eastern* to carry 4,000 passengers and a crew of 500, with the idea of bringing thousands of wealthy Americans to visit the upcoming French exposition, and $500,000 and four months had been spent converting the vessel for this purpose.[4]

---

2. A later version of this story was retitled "Un drame dans les airs" ("A Drama in the Air") for inclusion in the book *Le Docteur Ox*, published by Hetzel in 1874.

3. Doug Stewart, "There was too much Jonah in Brunel's Hapless Leviathan," *Smithsonian*, 25 (November 1994), 66. For more background on the *Great Eastern*, see James Dugan, *The Great Iron Ship* (New York: Harper & Brothers, 1956).

4. The crew was composed of nine nautical officers, three pursers, two surgeons, 17 petty officers, ten quartermasters, 79 seamen, 16 engineers, two boilermakers, two blacksmiths, one tin and coppersmith, 25 petty officers, 155 firemen, one engineers' clerk, two chief stewards, two seconds, two bar-keepers, four stewardesses, three bakers, and 90 stewards. "The Latest Passage of the Great Eastern" (letter from Paul du Chaillu), *Press* (New Zealand), XII, July 12, 1867, p. 3.

ARRIVAL OF THE STEAMSHIP "GREAT EASTERN" AT NEW YORK, April 8, 1867.—[See Page 270.]

The arrival of the *Great Eastern* in New York harbor.

Yet there were only 123 passengers on the westbound voyage, although the eastward return trip was expected to be full.[5] Verne traveled in the company of his brother and best friend, Paul, a mariner, and recounted his journey to America in *A Floating City* (*Une Ville flottante*, 1870), concentrating on the two-week voyage with only minor fictionalization; in particular, the last five chapters of the book are a largely factual account with only incidental narrative. The seemingly endemic bad luck of the *Great Eastern* delayed the journey both in port and at sea, truncating the visit to America by a week.

Jules and Paul left for Liverpool on March 16, and the sailing date was anticipated as March 23. However, there was a delay of three days on account of the difficulty of coaling in bad weather, during which the vessel's owners paid all necessary hotel bills for the passengers.[6] The voyage began tragically on March 26 with an accident as twelve men raised the half-ton port anchor, as contemporaneously described

5. See the listing in "Passengers Arrived," *Commercial Advertiser* (New York City), April 10, 1867, p. 4.

6. George S. Emmerson, *The Greatest Iron Ship—S.S. Great Eastern* (London: David & Charles, 1981), 135; "The Great Eastern," *The New-York Times*, April 9, 1867, p. 1.

by *The New York Times.*

> One of the capstan pins snapped, and the full weight of the anchor was suddenly thrown on the men, and of course overpowered them. The capstan was whirled round, throwing the men right and left, and the bars flying out, struck and wounded five men. One of them died immediately, and another was not expected to live.... The chief officer had a narrow escape; one of the capstan bars flew close to his head.[7]

This fatal incident itself only caused a delay of twenty minutes; Verne regarded it as a measure of the value of life in the Anglo-Saxon world.[8]

The next morning, passengers could admire the beautiful scenery of the Irish coast. Once into the broad Atlantic, the motion of the *Great Eastern* was perceptible; passing an abandoned ship, the wreck was tossed helplessly, with no signs of life upon her sinking deck. At sea, Paul Verne won popularity for his musical skill on the piano; there were five on board.[9] One of the travelers was Paul du Chaillu, the first white man to observe live gorillas, and he lectured twice, on "Ashangoland" where he had found pygmies, and on the natives of equatorial Africa.[10] An American wanted to speak on behalf of Mormonism, but the female passengers succeeded in convincing the captain, Sir James Anderson, to bar the presentation for fear it might entice the men toward the practice of polygamy.

The *Great Eastern* had placed two trans-Atlantic telegraph cables on the ocean floor, and Jules questioned the crew for details of nautical life and the creatures of the ocean depths, receiving ideas for the submarine novel he was planning that would become *Twenty Thousand Leagues under the Seas* (*Vingt Mille Lieues sous les mers*, 1870). Captain Anderson spoke one evening to the passengers, relating his experiences in laying the cable. The leader of the project, Cyrus Field, was also on board and a "celebrity," and Verne would name his

7. "The Sailing of the Great Eastern," *The New-York Times*, April 9, 1867, p. 1.

8. Emmerson, 136; "The Great Eastern," Jules Verne, *A Floating City and The Blockade Runners*, Translated by Henry Frith (London: George Routledge and Sons, 1883), Chapter 4.

9. "The Latest Passage of the Great Eastern."

10. "The Great Eastern."

heroic engineer in *The Mysterious Island*, Cyrus Smith, in honor of Field. In Verne's novel, despite the lack of the castaways having tools and supplies, Smith transforms the deserted Lincoln Island into a metaphor of the industrial revolution, through his knowledgeable use of raw materials.

On some days the weather allowed lounging on the luxurious deck, while at night the constellations could be observed.[11] However, several severe storms delayed the voyage by four days, and the engines had to be run slowly because some of the new parts tended to overheat. In one gale, the forward bulwarks were carried away, one man was seriously injured, and some five hundred tons of water came on deck, but the ship's buoyancy was unaffected.[12] While passing through the misty iceberg zone, Anderson navigated by drawing a bucket of fresh water every half-hour and checking its temperature to see if the sea was becoming colder. Passing close to an ice floe sent a chill felt all over the ship.[13]

On April 5, there was a storm and heavy seas, such as the sailors said they had never seen before, and for the the first time the *Great Eastern* shipped two great waves, and rolled considerably, but without damage. Calmer weather followed, and the next evening the sailors favored the passengers with a minstrel show. Sunday allowed the second Anglican Church service of the trip, which was held in the grand saloon of the *Great Eastern*. During the day, steamships voyaging eastward and bound for Europe began to pass more frequently.[14]

With the news of the ship's departure from Liverpool telegraphed to New York, there had been growing anxiety when the *Great Eastern* failed to appear at the expected time. Several false sightings had gathered crowds in anticipation of its arrival, only to disperse in disappointment. Finally, early the morning of April 8, a group of spectators cheered the ship near Sandy Hook Point and its lighthouse terminus, as the *Great Eastern* passed a flotilla of fishing vessels, and spectators massed to admire the passing leviathan.[15] Aboard, Verne scanned "the

11. "The Latest Passage of the Great Eastern."

12. "The Great Eastern."

13. "The Latest Passage of the Great Eastern."

14. "The Latest Passage of the Great Eastern."

15. "The Great Eastern."

green heights of New Jersey" on the one shore and, on the other, New York City stretching between the Hudson and East River.[16]

With the tide turning, the *Great Eastern* had to wait overnight before crossing the bar of the Hudson at noon and entering the river. It was the first time the *Great Eastern* had been in New York harbor in four years, and it was to be the ship's last visit there. Verne observed "The sea was enlivened by a fleet of yachts sailing along the coast." As the *Great Eastern* came to her moorings in the Hudson, the anchors fouled the telegraph cables of the river, which would have to be broken at the vessel's departure.[17]

The *Great Eastern* had been christened a "vast toy" by one of the Customs Inspectors at the West Street office who handled the ship's arrival on the North River. He was Herman Melville; his South Seas novels had found some acclaim, but his *Moby Dick* (1851) had yet to be recognized as a classic.[18] (In Verne's short story "The Humbug," ["Le Humbug", 1910] discussed below, one of the main characters is "Mrs. Melvil," whose husband is named Henri instead of Herman.) Curiously, Verne listed his occupation as lawyer, rather than author, on the passenger manifest for the *Great Eastern* logged by U.S. Customs on April 10, 1867, and preserved by the National Archives. Even more surprising, there are ditto marks beside Paul Verne's name, indicating the same profession as his brother.[19]

When the Vernes disembarked, they calculated that they had 192 hours—since the return aboard the *Great Eastern* was scheduled for April 16. This left a mere eight days, but Jules and Paul believed the time was sufficient if well deployed, to visit New York, the Hudson, the Valley of the Mohawk, Lake Erie, and Niagara. "A week! There are some rapid tourists, 'express travelers,' who would manage to 'do' the

16. *A Floating City and The Blockade Runners* (London: George Routledge and Sons, 1883), Chapter 34.

17. *A Floating City and The Blockade Runners* (London: George Routledge and Sons, 1883), Chapter 34. Additional contemporary accounts of the voyage appear in "The Great Eastern," *The World*, April 10, 1867, p. 1 and "The Great Eastern," *New York Daily Tribune*, April 10, 1867.

18. Stewart, 64.

19. <https://ia600301.us.archive.org/14/items/passengerlistsof0277unit/passengerlistsof0277unit.pdf>, accessed 12/31/2015, information provided by Stephen Michaluk, Jr. Jules and Paul Verne were listed along with the rest of the arrivals in "Passengers Arrived," *The New-York Times*, April 10, 1867.

The Vernes stayed at the Fifth Avenue Hotel.

whole of American in that time. I had no such pretensions, not even to visit New York seriously, and after this examination go and write a book upon the manners and customs of the American people."[20]

Checking into the Fifth Avenue Hotel, Jules and Paul evoked no interest. A fellow guest was named Professor Aronnax, newly arrived from the Nebraska Badlands, two details Verne would remember when writing *Twenty Thousand Leagues under the Seas.*

The city itself was walked until evening.

> It has no more variety than a chess-board. The streets, which intersect at right angles, are denominated "avenues" when they are longitudinal, and "streets" when they are transversal. The numbering of those roads is a very practical but very monotonous disposition of things; omnibuses traverse all the avenues.... A single artery obliquely intersects the symmetrical agglomeration of the quarters of New York, and carries life into them. This is the old Broadway, like the Strand in Lon-

20. *A Floating City and The Blockade Runners* (London: George Routledge and Sons, 1883), Chapter 35.

> don, or the Boulevard Montmartre in Paris, almost impassable at the lower end, where the crowd is thick, and almost deserted at the upper end. A street wherein marble palaces and shanties are mingled, a river of carriages, omnibuses, cabs, wagons, and drays, with pavements for its banks, and over which it has been found necessary to throw bridges to afford crossing to the foot passengers.

Jules added, "New York is a tongue of land," and at the southern extremity, the commercial population dwells.[21]

Dinner at the hotel was "a Lilliputian stew" served on "doll's plates."[22] Jules and Paul saw Barnum and Van Amburgh's Museum and a thrilling Dion Boucicault play, *The Streets of New York*. This story of "tough" youth in New York in the panic of 1857 featured a thrilling full-size fire engine battling a conflagration on stage in the final act.

The next evening the Vernes then crossed the East River and embarked on a crowded paddle steamer that only departed at night and was carrying more than 4,000 passengers, 1,500 of them immigrants, up the Hudson River. Jules described it as a house, rather than a boat, with "two or three rows of terraces, with galleries, verandas, and walking spaces." At the wheel house, four strong men held the spokes of the double wheel. "The two enormous paddle-boxes are painted in fresco, like the tympans of the Church of St. Mark at Venice. Behind each paddle-wheel rose a chimney from two furnaces … In the center, between the paddles, is the machinery of very simple construction: a single cylinder, a piston moving a large 'beam,' which rises and sinks like the immense hammer in a forge, and a single crank-shaft to communicate the movement to the wheels."[23]

They were soon enveloped in a thick fog, which allowed only a glimpse of the towns along the banks of the River, and in *A Floating City*, Verne compared the steamer's horn to the snorting of a mastodon in the gloom. The fog compelled the steamer to pause for five

21. *A Floating City and The Blockade Runners* (London: George Routledge and Sons, 1883), Chapter 35.

22. *A Floating City and The Blockade Runners* (London: George Routledge and Sons, 1883), Chapter 35.

23. *A Floating City and The Blockade Runners* (London: George Routledge and Sons, 1883), Chapter 36.

hours, and as a result, the Vernes were late arriving in Albany, forcing them to catch a train in the afternoon instead of the morning. This gave them time to explore the state capitol; to Jules it seemed like one of the quarters of New York City "had been transported to the side of the hill, upon which it rises like an amphitheater.... The lower town, commercial and populous, on the right bank of the Hudson; the upper town, with brick houses, public buildings, and a very remarkable museum of fossils."[24]

Verne had probably heard about the Cohoes Mastodon, the highlight of the museum. It had been discovered not far from Albany the previous autumn as the result of excavations for construction adjoining a river. The skeleton was remarkable for its condition, and was the second best preserved of its kind that had been found up to that time. However, at the time Verne saw it, the bones were piled in an apparent jumble, as shown in a sketch in the December 8, 1866 issue of *Harper's Weekly*, one of the most widely-circulated journals of the time.

Verne may have met Professor James Hall, head of the museum, and one of the most renowned figures in the nation in the field. He was New York's state geologist for fifty years, as famous for his bellicose, quarrelsome, and egotistical manner as for his scientific expertise. He was shortly to become embroiled in the notorious Cardiff Giant hoax, one of the most extraordinarily successful even in a time when they were common. George Hull, an atheist and student of Darwin, decided to test the limits of fundamentalist interpretations of the Bible, having heard a preacher maintain the literal truth of the line, "There were giants in the earth in those days" (Genesis 6:4). Hull created his own giant, a naked man of gypsum, modeled after himself but ten and a half feet tall, and weighing 3000 pounds, then arranged for it to be artificially aged and buried, to be dug up a year later, in 1869. It immediately began to attract spectators and was exhibited in New York City before Hull revealed the truth, and the incident received international press coverage.

Just as Verne's trip aboard the *Great Eastern* inspired him to write *A Floating City*, so too the accidental visit to the fossil museum in Albany, and the subsequent discovery of the Cardiff Giant, seems to have provided the inspiration for a story by Verne. In "The Humbug," a huckster with audacity exceeding Hull, claims to have unearthed bones of a pre-

24. *A Floating City and The Blockade Runners* (London: George Routledge and Sons, 1883), Chapter 36.

historic man some 120 feet tall. As in *A Floating City*, "The Humbug" is told through the first person narration of a Frenchman visiting America, who travels aboard a steamer from New York to Albany. This short story appears to have been written after Verne's trip to the United States and the discovery of the Cardiff Giant, although not published until 1910 by Jules's son and executor, Michel, in his posthumous anthology book, *Yesterday and Tomorrow* (*Hier et demain*). "The Humbug" is a logical extension of *A Floating City*; while that novel concentrates on other parts of Verne's sojourn in America, "The Humbug" embellishes his experience of the Hudson and Albany.[25]

After those crucial five hours in Albany, Paul and Jules Verne boarded a westward train.

> At one o'clock, having dined, we went to the railway station, an open terminus without barrier or officials. The train was waiting simply in the middle of the street, like an omnibus. People mounted into the long carriages when they pleased. These carriages are supported by four wheels at each end, and communicate with each other by bridges, which admit of the passengers walking from one extremity of the train to the other.... Instead of being boxed up, as in continental railways, we were free to move about as we pleased, to purchase newspapers and books ... At the hour named for our departure, without having seen guard or porter, without any bell ringing, without any notice ... started, and we proceeded at a rate of thirty-six miles an hour.[26]

Verne marveled at the scenery, crossing "woods newly thinned, at the risk of collision with the felled timber; through new cities, the streets of which were laid with rails, but to which houses were wanting still;" past cities "baptised with the most poetical names in ancient history—Rome, Syracuse, Palmyra."[27] The Mohawk Valley described by

25. For more on "The Humbug," see *Worlds Known and Unknown*, the upcoming final volume in the Palik series (Albany, GA: BearManor Fiction, 2017).

26. *A Floating City and The Blockade Runners* (London: George Routledge and Sons, 1883), Chapter 36.

27. *A Floating City and The Blockade Runners* (London: George Routledge and Sons, 1883), Chapter 36.

Cataract House.

James Fenimore Cooper's Leatherstocking Tales glided before their eyes; Cooper's books had been available in French translations since Verne's youth and were among his favorites.[28] (Over a quarter-century later he would remark, "I never tire of Fenimore Cooper; cer-

28. Ironically, both of the translations of *A Floating City* at the time, by Sampson Low and Scribner, Armstrong in 1874, and the later version by Routledge, apparently lacked the expected familiarity with Cooper's famous literary heroes featured in five novels published between 1823 and 1841. Natty Bumppo's nickname is Hawkeye in *The Last of the Mohicans*, but his appellation changes in each of the books; his Mohican friend is Chingachgook. Rather than referring back to Cooper's texts, in Chapter 36 both editions of *A Floating City* attempted to re-translate Hawkeye's name (given as Œil-de-Faucon in French) back into English, with different, amusing results in each version. The French text had incorrectly given Chingachgook's name as Chingagook, which the Routledge text failed to correct, while this was amended in the Sampson Low / Scribner, Armstrong version.

The American and Canadian Falls, with Goat Island between them.

tain of his romances deserve true immortality, and will I trust be remembered long after the so-called literary giants of a later age are forgotten."[29])

Jules and Paul changed trains at Rochester at 11 p.m., arriving at Niagara well past midnight. Rapids poured in cascades under the train. Early in the morning, they checked into "a magnificent hotel," Cataract House.[30]

Jules would describe their destination, 300 miles from Albany, in his familiar educative tone. The town of Niagara Falls

> enjoys salubrious air and a charming situation, with excellent hotes and comfortable villas, much frequented both by Yankees and Canadians during the summer….
>
> Niagara is not a river, not even a stream—it is a simple weir, a natural trench, a canal thirty-six miles long, which carries the waters from Lake Superior, Michigan, Huron, and Erie into Ontario. The difference in the level of these

29. Jules Verne in Marie A. Belloc, "Jules Verne at Home," *Strand Magazine*, 9 (Feb. 1895), 207-213.

30. *A Floating City and The Blockade Runners* (London: George Routledge and Sons, 1883), Chapter 36.

> two last lakes is 340 feet; this difference, if equally distributed throughout the whole course, would scarcely form a "rapid," but the falls alone take more than half the height, hence their grandeur.
>
> This Niagara canal divides the United States from Canada. The right bank is the American side, the left is British.[31]

Awakening on April 12, the sun was bright, and "a dull distant roar broke upon the ear, and I could perceive on the horizon some vapor which was not a cloud." On the Canadian side, there were a few little hills, houses and some bare trees. At the bank of the river, "the water was flowing calmly along, clear and not deep. Numerous points of grey rock rose up at intervals. The noise of the falls became more distinct, but we could not yet see them.... Upwards the river extended as far as we could see; downstream, to our right, we could perceive the first symptoms of a rapid, then ... the land suddenly sunk away and clouds of spray were held in the air in suspension."[32]

Jules and Paul walked a few hundred yards across a wooden bridge to Goat Island. Situated in the middle of the Niagara Falls, Goat Island is "a morsel of land about seventy acres in extent, covered with trees intersected by paths in which carriages can be driven, cast like a bouquet between the American and Canadian falls, which are 300 yards apart."[33] From it they saw "the turn of the Niagara upon itself [which] favors the effects of light and shade in a singular manner. The sun striking the waters at so many different angles changes their colors most capriciously ... Near Goat Island the foam is white, a pure snowy layer, a mass of molten silver falling into the void. In the center of the cataract they are of a beautiful sea-green tint, which proves the depth of the water ... Towards the Canadian side, again, the foaming masses, like metal beneath the sun's rays, shine brightly ... Beneath the fall the river is invisible; the spray rises over it in thick masses. I could nevertheless perceive enormous ice-blocks, de-

---

31. *A Floating City and The Blockade Runners* (London: George Routledge and Sons, 1883), Chapter 37.

32. *A Floating City and The Blockade Runners* (London: George Routledge and Sons, 1883), Chapter 37.

33. *A Floating City and The Blockade Runners* (London: George Routledge and Sons, 1883), Chapter 37.

A wintry view from Goat Island.

posited by the frosts of winter … Half a mile below the Falls the river is smooth again …."[34]

They traversed a rickety bridge to Terrapin Tower, placed in 1833 on the edge of a trembling rock some one hundred feet from the shore of Goat Island on the Canadian or "Horse-shoe" side. "I saw a bridge, or rather some planks, thrown across the rocks, which connected the tower with the bank of the river. This bridge crossed the abyss at the height of a few feet only, the torrent roared beneath. We ventured upon these planks, and in a few moments we had reached the principal rock upon which Terrapin Tower stands."[35] Forty-five feet in height, built of stone, with a circular wooden staircase inside, the tower had a landing and balcony. As Jules explained,

34. *A Floating City and The Blockade Runners* (London: George Routledge and Sons, 1883), Chapter 37.

35. *A Floating City and The Blockade Runners* (London: George Routledge and Sons, 1883), Chapter 37.

Terrapin Tower.

> Once at the top of the tower, you have only to hold tight and look around you.... From the summit the eye pierces to the depths of the abyss .... One can feel the shaking of the rock that supports the tower.... One cannot hear oneself speak. The roar of the water is like thunder.... The spray rises to the summit of the tower, and there forms a magnificent rainbow.
>
> By a simple optical effect, the tower appears to be moving with terrific speed, but in the contrary direction to the fall, for with the opposite effect it would be impossible to look at the fall without feeling giddy.[36]

After dinner at the Cataract House, the Vernes visited the "Three Sisters," islets at the head of Goat Island, allowing a view of the upper rapids. The Falls, still laden with ice, were particularly beautiful at sunset. All day Verne wandered these areas, viewing "the raging torrent" from every point, finding the best view of the American falls from the Canadian side. Jules noted that "the moon shone brightly. The shadow of the tower was cast upon the abyss." Walking until midnight, they were "irresistibly attracted" to the tottering Terrapin Tower.[37] (As Verne

36. *A Floating City and The Blockade Runners* (London: George Routledge and Sons, 1883), Chapter 37.

37. *A Floating City and The Blockade Runners* (London: George Routledge and Sons, 1883), Chapter 37.

The Suspension Bridge.

predicted, years later the imperceptibly receding falls would eventually cause Terrapin Tower to fall into them itself.) At the summit of the tower they remained, observing the half-light of a train two miles away emerging out of the gloom, while the moonbeams struck the dust-like foam, a lunar rainbow emerging in the night through the spray.

The following morning, the Vernes crossed the Suspension Bridge, the only one giving access from New York state to Canada. There were two levels, trains on the upper level and carriages and pedestrians below. At 800 feet long, it was supported by 4,000 wires with a diameter of ten inches. Reaching the center, a train passed overhead, "and we could feel the platform bend beneath our feet."[38]

Table Rock was a promontory a few yards square jutting out just below the falls over the river. While awaiting breakfast at the elegant English hotel, Clifton House, Verne scanned the Table Rock Album, the "Traveller's Book" wherein he noticed many names of international renown, from P.T. Barnum to Louis Napoleon. Most who came here in the 19th century signed their names, often jotting personal impressions of Niagara. Then Paul and Jules signed their own names.[39]

38. *A Floating City and The Blockade Runners* (London: George Routledge and Sons, 1883), Chapter 38.

39. The "Traveller's Book," dozens of separate volumes signed by visitors over the years, was housed in the Niagara Falls Museum. The Museum was originally owned by Thomas Barnett, as his own cabinet of curiosities; Barnett was the same man who owned the facilities at Table Rock at the time of Verne's visit. Established in 1827, the Museum

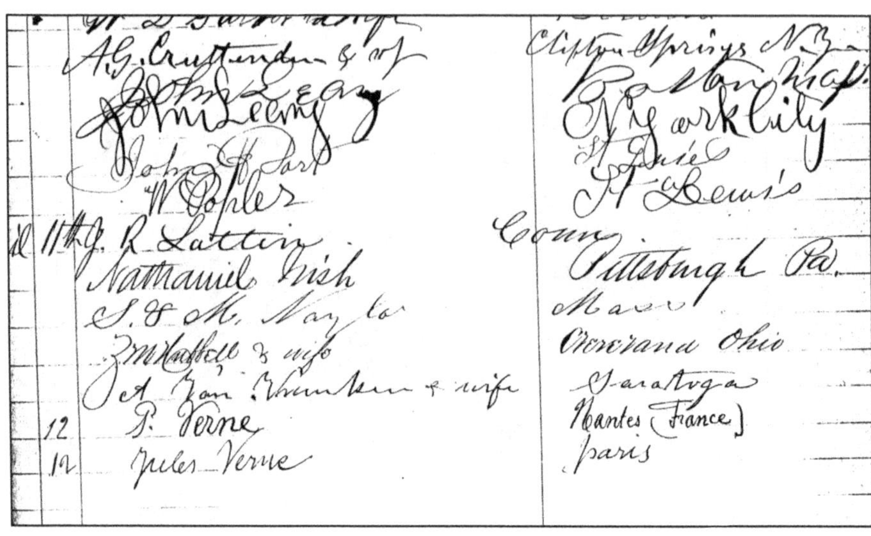

12	P. Verne	Nantes (France)
12	Jules Verne	paris

The page in the "Traveller's Book" signed by Jules and Paul.

Descent to "the Grotto of Winds," hollowed out beneath the central fall, was not allowed because of the frequent falling of the rocks. Jules and Paul were outfitted in waterproof garments to go under the falls by way of Barnett's Staircase, a long, slippery descent considered to be sufficiently perilous that a certificate was signed and issued Thomas Barnett.

> Thence, amid the spray, we passed behind the great fall. The cataract fell before us as the curtain in a theater descends before the actors. But what a theater! And how the air, violently displaced, came rushing in strong currents. Wet to the skin,

offered a cross-section of objects, from the remains of a mastodon (present at the time of Verne's visit) to Egyptian mummies (brought in 1860) and freaks of nature, weapons and armor, to vehicles used by daredevils who plunged over the falls. The Museum itself moved several times over the years, shifting from the Canadian to the American side, and was in its third location at the time of Verne's visit. There the album containing Paul and Jules Verne's signature was discovered by proprietor Jacob Sherman in 1997, working from information supplied by Stephen Michaluk, Jr., and went on display. Stephen Michaluk, Jr., "Niagara Falls and the Table Rock Album," *Autograph Times* (February, 1997), 15. Some Verne enthusiasts were lucky enough to see that "Traveler's Book" during the brief time before it was lost again, when in 1999 the Niagara Falls Museum was sold to a private collector.

Table Rock.

Clifton House.

> blinded, and nearly deaf, we could neither hear nor see anything in this cavern, as hermetically sealed by the cataract as if Nature had shut it up by a granite wall.[40]

Arriving at the banks of the river, covered by sheets of ice, they boarded a vessel which would take them back from the Canadian to the American side. When a mechanically-minded Kentucky engineer deplored the waste of energy at the falls, Verne wrote in *A Floating City* that he was inclined to throw him in the river.[41]

On April 14, Verne took a boat back to the American shore of Niagara, departing from there for New York City and his trip home. An express took the Vernes to Buffalo by early afternoon, where they spent several hours and tasted the water of Lake Erie. Changing trains the next morning at Albany, the Hudson Railroad returned the brothers to New York City in a few hours. Staying again at the Fifth Avenue Hotel, Verne saw more of the city, from the East River and Brooklyn, and the next day, April 16th, Jules and Paul once more boarded the *Great Eastern* for the return trip.

Of the thousands of Americans expected to make the trip to France, only 191 passengers were aboard; the fourteen days required on the voyage to New York was another factor discouraging bookings for the trip.[42] Twelve days later the Vernes arrived back in France, on May 1, Jules returning to his family and his own modest yacht, the *Saint-Michel*, two days later. The French press had tactfully omitted any mention of the return voyage of the *Great Eastern* to save Napoleon embarrassment, but the *New York Times* estimated that the voyage had lost $100,000. The crew were never paid, nor were the contractors who had refitted the ship, nor did Napoleon fulfill his promised reimbursement of the English backers. Not until 1870 was Verne's novel about the trip, *A Floating City*, published in France, in *Journal des débats politiques et littéraires*, with hardback appearance the following year; it was translated into English in 1874. *A Floating City* was accompanied by the American Civil War novella, *The Blockade Runners*, in both English and French.

40. *A Floating City and The Blockade Runners* (London: George Routledge and Sons, 1883), Chapter 38.

41. *A Floating City and The Blockade Runners* (London: George Routledge and Sons, 1883), Chapter 39.

42. Emmerson, 137.

The Grotto of Winds.

Under the Falls.

Frontispiece for *A Floating City*.

The rapids above the Falls.

Verne was deeply moved by the sight of Niagara, and its memory proved so durable that over twenty years later he laid pivotal episodes of two novels there. The hero and heroine in *Family without a Name* go over the cataract in a fiery ship, the *Caroline*, based on an 1837 historical incident. As a reprisal against rebels, Canadian loyalists burned their vessel, and killed one of the crew, although in fact the *Caroline* burned in the river, rather than going over the precipice. In *Master of the World* (*Maître du monde*, 1904), Robur takes the *Terror* to the end of Niagara Falls, but instead of plunging with the waters, he flies out of them, into the air, by transforming the *Terror* from a ship into an airplane. In fact, the rocks in the rapids would have made a safe voyage through them impossible; both the American and Canadian falls are strewn with boulders and lack the depth necessary for the *Terror* or the *Caroline* to pass. However, the idea was already present in *A Floating City*, where Verne noted how a ship drawing twenty feet of water had been launched into the current and descended the falls without having been blocked by the rocks.[43]

43. *A Floating City and The Blockade Runners* (London: George Routledge and Sons, 1883), Chapter 37.

The destruction of the American steamer *Caroline* by the British was recounted in *Family Without a Name.*

The *Terror* flies out of Niagara Falls in *Master of the World.*

Verne regretted the short period in the United States, abbreviated by the delays of the *Great Eastern*; he calculated the five days as 192 hours. As he exclaimed, "What could I do? I had a ticket to go and come which was only good for a week!" Verne hoped to return to the United States someday, until finally advancing age and ill-health made such a trip impossible. *A Floating City*, *Family without a Name*, and *Master of the World* serve as permanent reminders of the lifelong influence of that 1867 journey by Verne.

Illustrations

One of the challenges in the Palik series is selecting illustrations. They are either derived from the first French publication of Verne stories in the 19th century and the beginning of the 20th century, or selected from sources of the time depicting actual historical locales, persons or events. Illustrations for *The Castles of California* are from the original publication in *Musée des Familles* (save for one engraving of the gold fields), and those for *A Nephew from America* from an early Italian edition. The illustrations of Verne's trip to America are authentic views of the time.

For illustrations from the original publications of Verne, the North American Jules Verne Society is indebted to Bernhard Krauth, chairman of the German Jules-Verne-Club. Intensely interested in the illustrations of the original French editions of Verne's work, he has been deeply involved in a project to digitize the illustrations, more than 5,000 in all.

Many of the additional illustrations were provided by renowned Verne biographer Volker Dehs, to whom the North American Jules Verne Society is indebted for advice and assistance in the Palik series.

The cover is a classic and widely-reprinted design from Czechoslovakian editions, and the scan was provided by Jan Rychlík especially for this Palik series volume.

Acknowledgements

The Palik series, while spearheaded by the North American Jules Verne Society, represents a cooperative effort among Vernians worldwide, pooling the resources and knowledge of the various organizations in different countries. The Society is grateful for research assistance to Frédéric Jaccaud, curator of Jean-Michel Margot's Verne Collection at the Maison d'Ailleurs (House of Elsewhere) in Yverdon-les-Bains, Switzerland.

The City of Nantes (France) and its Municipal Library have placed all Jules Verne manuscripts online. They helped make this publication possible, and the Society would like to thank the City of Nantes and its Bibliothèque municipale (Agnès Marcetteau, director) for their ongoing assistance with the Palik Series.

The Society also appreciates the efforts of members who have contributed to this volume, especially Jean-Michel Margot, and Stephen Michaluk, Jr. Proofreading and dramatic format advice was provided by David March and Alex Kirstukas. Further assistance has been provided by Jean Frodsham, Elvira Berkowitsch, and Pachara Yongvongpaibul.

Contributors

Kieran O'Driscoll was awarded his Ph.D. in Verne literary translation by Dublin City University, in 2010. His doctoral thesis was entitled *Around the World in Eighty Changes: A Diachronic Study of Six Complete Translations (1873-2004), From French to English, of Jules Verne's Novel, Le Tour du Monde en Quatre-Vingts Jours (1873)*, and explored the multiple causes of Verne retranslations. The monograph version was titled *Retranslation through the Centuries: Jules Verne in English*, published in 2011 by Peter Lang Ltd. Kieran holds a B.A. in Applied Languages (French and Spanish) with International Marketing Communications (2003) from Waterford Institute of Technology, and an M.A. in Translation Studies (2005) from Dublin City University, both degrees with First Class Honors. His Master's dissertation focused on the translations into French of J.K. Rowling's Harry Potter series. He has lectured in French at third-level, and in Advanced English as a Foreign Language, and has also done professional literary translation. Before entering academia, Kieran worked for almost twenty years in Irish local government, and also holds academic qualifications in Public Administration, Law and Music (Pianoforte). For the Palik Series, O'Driscoll has also translated Vice, *Redemption, and the Distant Colony*; *Golden Danube*; and portions of *The Marriage of a Marquis* and *Worlds Known and Unknown.*

Brian Taves (Ph.D., University of Southern California) has been an archivist in the Motion Picture, Broadcasting, and Recorded Sound Division of the Library of Congress since 1990. He is the author of over 100 articles and 25 chapters in anthologies. Taves has also written books on P.G. Wodehouse and Hollywood; director Robert Florey; the genre of historical adventure movies; and fantasy-adventure writer

Talbot Mundy, in addition to editing an original anthology of Mundy's best stories. In 2002-2003, Taves was chosen as Kluge Staff Fellow at the Library to write the first book on silent film pioneer Thomas Ince, published in 2011. In 2015, Taves's *Hollywood Presents Jules Verne: The Father of Science Fiction on Screen* was published by University Press of Kentucky. Taves was coauthor of *The Jules Verne Encyclopedia* (Scarecrow, 1996), and editor of the first English-language publication of Verne's *Adventures of the Rat Family* (Oxford, 1993), before becoming editor of the Palik series.

The Palik Series

The last two decades have brought astonishing progress in the study of Jules Verne, with new translations of Verne stories, including the discovery of many texts. Still, there remain a number of Verne stories that have been overlooked, and it is this gap that the North American Jules Verne Society seeks to fill in the Palik series.

The North American Jules Verne Society (NAJVS) was formed in 1993, and a decade later, underwrote *Journey Through the Impossible*, the first complete edition in any language of Verne's 1882 science fiction theatrical spectacle, *Voyage à travers l'impossible*. With this experience, and thanks to the generosity of the Society's late member, Edward Palik, a series was commenced to bring to the Anglophone public a series of hitherto unknown Verne tales, published by Bear-Manor Fiction.

Edward D. Palik (1928-2009) was a physicist who had a special enthusiasm for bringing neglected Verne stories to English-speaking readers, and this will be reflected in the series that bears his name. In this way the Society hopes to fulfill the goal that Ed's consideration has made possible, along with the assistance of a variety of Verne translators and scholars from around the world. The volumes in the Palik series will reveal the amazing range of Verne's storytelling, in genres that may surprise those who only know his most famous stories. We hope to allow a better appreciation of the famous writer who has, for more than a century and a half, been the widest-read author of fiction in the world.

Previous Volumes in the Palik Series

The Marriage of a Marquis

Foreword by Brian Taves; Introduction by Walter James Miller; *The Marriage of Mr. Anselme des Tilleuls* translated by Edward Baxter, with a preface and notes by Jean-Michel Margot; afterword by Edward Baxter; Appendix: *Jédédias Jamet, or The Tale of an Inheritance* translated, with a preface and annotations, by Kieran M. O'Driscoll.

Jules Verne is the acclaimed author of such pioneering science fiction as *Twenty Thousand Leagues under the Seas* and *Journey to the Center of the Earth*. Yet he also wrote much more, and foreshadowing such classics as *Around the World in Eighty Days*, this inaugural volume focuses on two of Verne's earliest humorous stories, *The Marriage of Mr. Anselme des Tilleuls* and *Jédédias Jamet, or The Tale of an Inheritance*. Mr. Anselme des Tilleuls, in the featured story, is a ridiculous young man seeking a bride, following the advice of his Latin tutor to utilize the maxims of that language in his courtship. Translation is provided by Edward Baxter and Kieran O'Driscoll, two of the leading Verne experts; critical commentary by Jean-Michel Margot, Walter James Miller, and Brian Taves examine both stories, and why some of the author's tales were overlooked for so many years.

Shipwrecked Family: Marooned with Uncle Robinson

Translated by Sidney Kravitz; Introduction by Brian Taves.

Castaway by pirates on a deserted island … without tools or supplies to survive … a mother and her children have only a kindly old sailor to help. But what explains the strange flora and fauna they find?

The second volume in the Palik series was rejected by Verne's publisher, so rather than finish it, he began to rewrite it with new characters—and that became the classic, *The Mysterious Island*, where Captain Nemo made his last appearance. Here, then, is Verne's first draft of that novel, one which is very different from the book that it became.

Translation is provided by Sidney Kravitz, also translator of the definitive modern edition of *The Mysterious Island* (Wesleyan University Press, 2002). The introduction by Brian Taves discusses the influence of the Robinsonade on Verne's oeuvre, while an appendix comprises Verne's own prefaces to two of his novels in the genre, describing the influence of the form on his writing.

Mr. Chimp & Other Plays

By Jules Verne with Michel Carré, Charles Wallut, and Victorien Sardou; Translated by Frank Morlock; Introduction by Jean-Michel Margot.

Long before Verne stories had formed the basis for such movies as *Around the World in 80 Days*, many of his plays were theatrical blockbusters on the 19th century stage, including several from his novels. Even as he became a novelist, the stage remained crucial to Verne. In this volume, expert scholarly research by Jean-Michel Margot introduces four of Verne's plays written early in his career, from 1853 to 1860. The four plays are translated by Frank Morlock, one of the most prolific modern translators of 19th century French drama. Included in this volume are: *The Knights of the Daffodil* and *Mr. Chimpanzee*, co-authored by Verne with Michel Carré; *An Adoptive Son*, co-authored by Verne with Charles Wallut, and *Eleven Days of Siege*, co-authored by Verne with Charles Wallut and Victorien Sardou. The works range in content from romantic comedies to a scientist's discovery that there may not be much difference between human and ape after all!

The Count of Chanteleine: A Tale of the French Revolution

Translated by Edward Baxter; Introduction by Brian Taves; Notes and maps by Garmt de Vries-Uiterweerd; Afterword by Volker Dehs.

This adventure, first published in France in 1864 but never before available in English, is for everyone who has thrilled to *The Scarlet Pim-*

pernel, A Tale of Two Cities, or *Scaramouche*. A nobleman, the Count of Chanteleine, leads a rebellion against the revolutionary French government. While he fights for the monarchy and the church, his home is destroyed and his wife murdered by the mob. Now he must save his daughter from the guillotine. This exciting swashbuckler is also a meticulous historical re-creation of a particularly bloody episode in the Reign of Terror.

Commentary by an international team of experts including Garmt de Vries-Uiterweerd, Volker Dehs and Brian Taves explores the historical background, composition, and generic context of *The Count of Chanteleine*, translated by Edward Baxter.

The Count of Chanteleine is also available in a full-length professional reading by the noted vocal artist, Fred Frees, on audible.com.

Vice, Redemption and the Distant Colony

By Jules Verne with Michel Verne; *Pierre-Jean*, *The Somber Fate of Jean Morénas*, and *Fact-Finding Mission* translated, with an introduction and annotations, by Kieran M. O'Driscoll

Literary fraud or filial devotion? This is the question at the heart of a firestorm that erupted when manuscripts and letters were discovered proving that Jules Verne's son, Michel, significantly revised over a dozen of the stories published posthumously under his father's name, and even originated some himself. It was a collaboration that had begun while both were still alive, and continued as Michel was his father's literary executor.

In this volume will be found two different versions of a story, as written by Jules (*Pierre-Jean*), and expanded by his son (into *The Somber Fate of Jean Morénas*)—a tale Michel even made as a full-length movie in 1916. Also in these pages is the first English translation of a novel Jules began, *Fact-Finding Mission*, but which his son finished, and hitherto has been only available in the completed version by Michel Verne.

The English rendering and notes are by a leading Verne translator and expert on the history of Verne translations, Kieran O'Driscoll.

Around the World in 80 Days—The 1874 Play

By Jules Verne and Adolphe d'Ennery; The original translation commissioned by the Kiralfy Brothers; Introduction by Philippe Burgaud, with Jean-Michel Margot and Brian Taves; Afterword: "The Meridians and the Calendar" by Jules Verne, translated and annotated by Jean-Louis Trudel; Appendix: The Play on Screen, by Brian Taves.

Jules Verne's most famous novel was originally conceived as a play—and immediately after writing the novel, Verne himself adapted his story into a stage hit. Running for thousands of performances in many different countries, including the United States, here is the original playscript, translated directly from the French by the producers of the original Broadway presentation, and only issued in the most limited form in 1874. Like filmmakers after him, Verne understood the need to make changes for the stage, and in collaboration with Adolphe d'Ennery created a distinct variation, a play with many different characters and episodes than are in the novel, *Around the World in Eighty Days*. Included in this volume are an introduction about how the play was created and staged, together with the first translation of Verne's 1873 essay, "The Meridians and the Calendar," (by Jean-Louis Trudel) explaining how Phileas Fogg accomplished his feat. Background on the production of the play, especially its staging in the United States, is provided by Philippe Burgaud, Jean-Michel Margot, and Brian Taves, along with an appendix on films of the play.

Bandits & Rebels

San Carlos and *The Siege of Rome* translated by Edward Baxter; With "Future of the Submarine;" Introduction by Daniel Compère, translated by Jean-Michel Margot with Brian Taves; Appendix: *Martin Paz, or The Pearl of Lima*, the 1852 translation by Anne T. Wilbur of the original French magazine edition.

Captain Nemo's *Nautilus* in *Twenty Thousand Leagues under the Seas* was not the first undersea craft imagined by Jules Verne! A decade earlier, the prophetic author wrote *San Carlos*, imagining a Spanish smuggler who utilizes a vehicle capable of diving beneath the surface of the waves. This newly-discovered story is published here in English for the first time—together with Verne's final words before his death on the future of the submarine as an instrument of war. Also in this volume is another never-before-translated tale, *The Siege of Rome*, a historical adventure of love and betrayal as Garibaldi's revolutionaries are defeated in 1849. Sorbonne professor Daniel Compère introduces the expert translations by Edward Baxter.

Since *Bandits & Rebels* emphasizes two Verne stories written early in his career, but remained unpublished during his lifetime, this volume also includes *Martin Paz*, another story of the same genre but which did appear in the 1850s, in both France and the United States. Reprinted here for the first time from the original translation, this preserves in unvarnished form Verne's own first version of *Martin Paz* to American readers. Previously, only the more polished version rewritten in the 1870s has appeared in book form.

Golden Danube

Translated, with an introduction and annotations, by Kieran M. O'Driscoll.

Jules Verne's "Extraordinary Journeys" often used the travelogue mode, and here the author offers a voyage down the entire length of the Danube, from Germany to the Black Sea. However, rather than the placid "blue" Danube of classical conception, the author offers one which is golden, in multiple ways. Smugglers are operating along the river, with the police in pursuit, and the hero is a champion fisherman who is abducted and forced to prove his courage.

The English rendering and notes are by a leading Verne translator and expert on the history of Verne translations, Kieran O'Driscoll.

A Priest in 1835

Translated with an introduction and notes, by Danièle Chatelain and George Slusser

Here is not only a treasure, but a literary revelation—the very first novel by Jules Verne. Finished by the age of 20 and under the influence of Edgar Allan Poe, *A Priest in 1835* was composed before Verne encountered any editors to hone his storytelling skills. Yet this tyro effort is a masterpiece, a novel told in a modernist style with a nonlinear narrative. This first English translation, with extensive critical commentary, redeems *A Priest in 1835* from the neglect and misunderstanding of French critics, who mistook its contemporary approach for an unfinished work. Instead, Verne reveals that he had not only the prophetic skills that would render him the father of science fiction, but a technique that would win him a place among the vanguard of 21st century authors.

Danièle Chatelain (University of Redlands) and George Slusser (University of California, Riverside) are renowned translators and scholars of the early history of science fiction.

Additional volumes are underway.

In 2003, the North American Jules Verne Society also co-published (with Prometheus) the Verne play, ***Journey through the Impossible***. A tale of fantasy and science fiction, *Journey through the Impossible* ran for 97 performances in Paris in 1882 and 1883. In three acts, the characters go first to the center of the Earth, then under the sea, and finally into outer space to the imaginary extrasolar planet Altor. Characters from *Journey to the Center of the Earth*, *From the Earth to the Moon*, *Twenty Thousand Leagues under the Sea*, and *A Fancy of Doctor Ox* appear again in *Journey through the Impossible*. The players include Captain Nemo, the lunar travelers Barbicane and Michel Ardan, Doctor Ox, and Professor Lidenbrock, after his trip to the center of the earth. Translation of *Journey through the Impossible* is by Edward Baxter, with introduction and notes by Jean-Michel Margot, along with reviews from the play's first presentation. Roger Leyonmark provides new illustrations in the style of the 19th century woodcuts that first illustrated French editions of Verne works, and the original engravings from the play are also featured. This is both the first complete edition in any language and the first English translation of a surprising work, by the popular Frenchman whose writing continue to delight readers—and audiences—to this day.

For additional details, reviews, and links to order the books, see the North American Jules Verne Society's website, najvs.org.

The North American Jules Verne Society

Jules Verne was a Frenchman, born in Nantes in 1828, who lived most of his life in Amiens, where he passed away in 1905. Despite his nationality, Verne has always had an exceptional popularity among English-language readers, one which the North American Jules Verne Society celebrates today as the successor to previous organizations.

The first group of Verne enthusiasts was formed, not in Verne's own France, but in England. The Jules Verne Confederacy began in 1921 at Dartmouth Royal Naval College, publishing *Nautilus*, a literary magazine in tribute to Verne and his son Michel, with whom they were in regular contact until Michel's death in 1925. The most permanent legacy of the Confederacy came with the publication of the Everyman's Library edition of *Five Weeks in a Balloon and Around the World in Eighty Days* in 1926, reprinted as late as 1966. Not only did it contain some of the first new, corrected translations, but the introduction by members of the Confederacy offered one of the earliest thoughtful critical overviews and bibliographies of Verne.

In France, the Société Jules Verne was formed in 1935, but their work would be interrupted by war and did not resume until 1967. Meanwhile, the American Jules Verne Society began a 20-year association. It was initiated when Willis E. Hurd penned an article, "A Collector and His Jules Verne," for the August 1936 issue of *Hobbies*, recounting his discovery that most of Verne's novels available in English had received many different translations, under widely divergent titles. A number of enthusiasts read Hurd's pioneering analysis, and a network formed. Hurd's retirement allowed him to take an interest in authoring English versions of some of Verne's untranslated stories. His collection would be willed to the Library of Congress and the volumes of another American Jules Verne Society member, James C. Iradi, were deposited at Indiana University's Lilly Library. Iraldi was still active in the late 1960s when Ron Miller and Laurence Knight began the Dakkar Grotto, publishing two issues of a journal entitled *Dakkar*, after Captain Nemo's original Indian name.

In 1993, the North American Jules Verne Society (NAJVS) formed, and has steadily grown with annual meetings and a peer-reviewed newsletter, *Extraordinary Voyages*. Although founded largely by collectors, the group now includes scholars and readers generally, to span all types of Verne admirers. In 2003, NAJVS undertook its first book publication, Verne's science fiction play, *Journey through the Impossible*, with the Palik series of first-time translations commencing seven years later.

The Society is a not-for-profit corporation with these goals and objectives:

- To promote interest in Jules Verne and his writings.
- To provide a forum for the interchange of information and materials about and/or relating to Jules Verne and his works, such as annual meetings with workshops and presentations.
- To stimulate Jules Verne research.
- To publish a newsletter, *Extraordinary Voyages*, with articles about Jules Verne and Society related issues.

Information on membership and activities, along with various educational activities, may be found at the society's website, najvs.org, as well as on Facebook.

www.ingramcontent.com/pod-product-compliance
Lightning Source LLC
Chambersburg PA
CBHW060304100426
42742CB00011B/1862

* 9 7 8 1 6 2 9 3 3 1 2 6 3 *